T0116523

Pre-Board Praise for
The Road Warrior
After God's Own Heart

The Road Warrior After God's Own Heart *by Bryan Paul Buckley is a thoughtful and powerful devotional catered to the "Road Warrior." This is a 30-day devotional that doesn't end when the book is complete! It has provided me with tools that will last a lifetime and allows me to be victorious in the face of temptation and challenges while on the road. Putting these tools into action has been a game-changer not only for me, but for my family as well! I can 100% recommend* The Road Warrior After God's Own Heart *for anyone who travels."*

~Matthew Oakes, airline pilot.

As the Pastor of a large Chicago-land church, I have close relationships with congregants who are on the road due to their job. The challenges they face as Christians are unique and exceptionally difficult. Their desire to pursue God is hindered. Their weaknesses are exposed. They are oftentimes alone and bombarded with temptations. Unfortunately, I can't fully relate and until now I've lacked the resources to support them. While much has been written about the life of King David, Bryan Paul Buckley provides a biblical and compelling comparison to today's traveling businessperson. I've seen this modeled in Bryan's life and under his leadership at our church. Thanks to this book, believers are able to draw near to God despite being far from home. Every pastor needs to gift this book to the road warriors in their church!

~Jon Kalvig, Pastor at The Compass Church

Bryan Buckley is the real deal. He has not just read books about what it is like to live life on the road or talked to businesspeople about it, he has lived it. I've traveled with him and have seen him live it out. He knows what it is to leave early on a Monday morning to come back on a Thursday evening to kids who want his attention, a wife who is tired from doing family on her own, and a company needing the work to get done. The Road Warrior After God's Own Heart *is a book to inspire, to encourage, to remind you* that you are not alone, and that you have a God who loves you and is for you. This is a book you want with you as you travel from city to city trying to love God, family, and navigate your life.

If you're a follower of Jesus trying to navigate the adventure and the dangers of life on the road you won't want to leave this book behind. We know the temptations that come being away from family and the loneliness that can set in. This book reminds us that we have a God who loves us and never gives up on us. Don't give up on what God has for you!

This book has helped me navigate those moments on the road. From navigating the temptations, to having friends pray for me, to loving my wife and kids, and trying to eat healthy this book will help every aspect of your life.

~Pastor Ronn Smith, Compass Church

"Having known each other since childhood, Bryan and I have been each other's David and Jonathan. Our brotherhood was most often demonstrated in the challenging times in life. In this book Bryan brings the familiar and maybe not so familiar stories of King David into a unique new light. HIs raw honesty and passion will challenge you to develop your faith in both the highs and lows of life. Every business person can grow from embracing this book both on and off the road".

~Rod Massie, VP of Sales

A book to help and guide Christians who travel frequently is a much-needed resource in our current culture. Managing the priorities of devoting time and effort to God, family, and professional success is a difficult multifaceted feat to achieve. As an airline pilot for nearly 25 years, I find this topic highly relevant in my own life on the road. This book discusses various aspects of David's life to apply in the lives of travelers like me. Just like David, we are all imperfect humans, but God has a plan for us! Life as a road warrior can be tough, but this book helps guide our path down that road!

~Jason King, airline pilot

What a wonderful book, and fantastic reminder of the power God has in our lives -- at home and away!! In today's world there is an immense amount of pressure on everyone to be the best version of themselves and to still juggle all *of the commitments that bring our life color. As a Christian, the pressure is amplified because we don't want to disappoint God, our family, our company, and the list goes on and on. This book is a beautiful reminder and a wonderful guide on how to navigate the unique pressures that are placed on us, by referencing scripture to give us guidance and keep our eyes focused on our faith.*

~Jennifer Prout, Verizon technical team
leader, road warrior, and mother

Also by Bryan Paul Buckley

The Elite Road Warrior:
Six Energy Habits to Master the Business Travel Life

Elite Business Travel Boss:
The Unwritten Success Guide for Leading Business Travel Teams

THE ROAD WARRIOR

AFTER GOD'S OWN HEART

BRYAN PAUL BUCKLEY

WESTBOW
PRESS®
A DIVISION OF THOMAS NELSON
& ZONDERVAN

WestBow Press books may be ordered through booksellers or by contacting:

WestBow Press
A Division of Thomas Nelson & Zondervan
1663 Liberty Drive
Bloomington, IN 47403
www.westbowpress.com
844-714-3454

ISBN: 979-8-3850-0662-5 (sc)
ISBN: 979-8-3850-0661-8 (e)

Library of Congress Control Number: 2023918303

Print information available on the last page.

WestBow Press rev. date: 09/23/2023

To the Spiritual Road Warrior

This book is dedicated to the Christian business traveler—those who are out there in the throes of temptations that are unknown to those who *don't* travel for work.

I see you. I *am* you.

And this book is designed specifically for you, to bring you perspective, hope, and encouragement every single day you choose to seek to become a road warrior after God's own heart.

If I can be an encouragement to you in any way, you have my permission to reach out to me directly:

Bryan@EliteRoadWarrior.com
630.689.7606

CONTENTS

FOREWORD

WHY THIS BOOK IS IMPORTANT TO YOU AS A ROAD WARRIOR

For over 18 years I have traveled professionally, providing coaching and leadership development seminars for Christian leaders across America and Canada. I am deeply grateful for the chance to help a large number of Christian leaders navigate their lives in more filling and effective ways. As a result, I am personally familiar with the incredible opportunities that can come with professional travel. I also am very familiar with the undeniable temptations and trials that also come along with being a road warrior. I know first-hand how difficult the struggle can be to stay loyal to our dearly-held values, when we are alone and unknown, far away from home.

The other major part of my professional life is centered around providing therapy and coaching for the same population of Christian leaders for over the past 20 years. A high percentage of those leaders travel consistently nationally and internationally. Additionally, my experience has given me opportunities to work with a range of other professionals who are road warriors—like Bryan—along with a few commercial pilots, who in some ways face even more intense temptations in their unique roles.

My professional experience working with these individuals has underscored, even more deeply, the rewards and risks of being a professional road warrior. Some of my clients discovered ways to thrive on the road. On the other hand, some marriages haven't made it. Some relationships with children haven't recovered. And some careers have blown up.

WHY THE LIFE OF DAVID IS IMPORTANT TO YOU AS A ROAD WARRIOR

All of the above underscores why this book is so important: it's validation to help you know that you're not alone as a road warrior, and to have some powerful insights, drawn from Bryan's own experience. More importantly, Bryan's rich framework for becoming a thriving road warrior is supported by the life of one of the most amazing and imperfect men in the history of the Bible, a man who in some ways was one of the first road warriors, none other than the iconic David.

David's life seemed to be lived in technicolor. Nearly everything he did and experienced seemed to be some kind of extreme. As Bryan deeply studied David's life, he discovered six illuminating categories for us a road warriors to understand in order to skillfully navigate the real range of experiences we are very likely to have on the road warrior's journey. Based on David's journey, Bryan helps us see how important cooperating with God's leading early on can be in helping us prepare for future opportunities, especially when we are unknown. Next, David's quick rise to fame as a warrior and Saul's brutal betrayal provides a launching point to help us be more prepared for corporate realities that are commonplace in today's corporate world.

Finding ways to navigate unexpected changes and the range of losses that come when we lose a job and related friendships can be overwhelming, if not devastating. Bryan masterfully draws on David's time as a loner and how he grew closer to God during a time of isolation from the world he knew.

David eventually becomes a very strong leader through the next season of his life, and through that experience, Bryan underscores some key insights that are valuable to helping us grow through David's leadership journey.

The most painful and regret-laden time of David's life, though, emerges when his struggles to show up as a husband and father become blatantly obvious. Bryan's distillation of lessons from that part of David's life provide a strong motivation for us to show up better in a hugely important part of our lives.

Lastly, Bryan provides a powerful reminder of the importance of "beginning with the end in mind" by looking at David's life from the vantage point of his legacy, and how David skillfully handled his own succession.

BUT WHY LISTEN TO BRYAN?

Well, first, I have an immense amount of respect for Bryan Paul Buckley.

I don't know if I'll ever forget the first day that I met him in church one Sunday morning over ten years ago. He was this engaging, bright, hip, and strong dude who was compelling in a godly way. (Sadly, I will never have Bryan's biceps.) Through the passage of time at church, more opportunities presented themselves to help me to get to know him better.

As our relationship has deepened, my respect for him has only grown. Bryan is a voracious reader and learner. He thinks deeply and is an excellent listener. Eventually, he would become a very close friend and someone who has let me into his story on deeper levels.

Bryan is certainly not perfect, yet *how he has responded* to his trials and sufferings (some of which he acknowledges were clearly of his own making) is perhaps the most impressive thing about him.

Seeing him grow and persevere through intense, and sometimes chronic, health and personal challenges has been simply inspiring.

To see how Bryan has incorporated an astute and actionable study of the life of David as a road warrior fills me with a deep joy.

Bryan has done a great job setting us up as readers to help us reflect and become more successful in our desire to become more like Jesus while we are away from the safety of our friendly confines. (Shout out to fellow Cubs fans!)

As you read this stellar devotional in short chunks of time, and apply it to your life, I believe it will reap lasting benefits. For your sake and for those you love dearly, I urge you to embrace what Bryan has worked so diligently to share.

Know that you are not alone when you head out on the road. You have the Holy Spirit inside you, and you have the cloud of witnesses around you. Plus, you have Bryan and my heart as well at your side in spirit praying for you to make the right choice at the right time to honor what matters most.

May this book truly help you become more like Jesus, the ultimate road warrior, and help you anticipate a rich welcome into your ultimate travel destination—the wondrous kingdom of heaven.

Nick Howard, Psy.D.
www.finishwellgroup.com

INTRODUCTION

WHY TEN MINUTES A DAY SHOULD MATTER TO YOU ON THE ROAD

The road. Those that travel for business—whether once in a while or on a consistent basis—know what I mean by the challenges of the road. You're always moving, always on, and always adjusting to travel and schedule changes. The road is hard: from staying in shape, eating healthy, and getting any rest to keeping up with work, connecting with your family back home, and just finding a few minutes to yourself to think and catch your breath.

Then you add the relentless distractions and temptations that only a road warrior knows and experiences. The evil one whispers everything from "Nobody will ever know" to "It's the cost of doing business to win or keep the deal, so it's okay, right?" The guilt, shame, and regret of the spiritual road warrior are all too often overwhelming and paralyzing.

My faith is important to me but on any given business trip, sadly, there's not as much evidence of that as I'd like. Most of the time, my only consistency was how *inconsistent* I was in taking the uninterrupted and focused time with God that I desperately needed. And of all places that I need to feel God's presence and be an influence on others, it's on a business trip!

> *One of my biggest challenges on the road is not only finding time alone with God, but specifically reading something that can relate to my life as a business traveler.*

There's just nothing out there that specifically addresses the faith of the business traveler, and believe me, I've looked high and low. I find myself having to curate, then translate content to the context of the road. I've longed to read something that makes me say, "that's me" and "they get my business travel world in a Christian context!"

But then I started reading about a Bible character I've read or heard about at church hundreds of times. This is a character I so wanted to be like in many ways—and avoid like the plague in other ways.

It's the iconic David.

To begin with, the Bible devotes more space to David than to any other character. Moses and Jesus rival him for sheer number of pages—until you add Psalms (of which David wrote at least half.) Then David wins hands down. Even without the Psalms, there is more about David's life than the lives of the other biblical characters.

"David is no lawgiver or teacher, but a man of deeds and actions. The David of the Bible is also a complex character. He is pious and faithful at times but is also capable of heinous crimes. He is a powerful and decisive man, except around his children, whom he cannot control."[1]

The story of David and Goliath strikes a powerful chord in all of us. It's perhaps the most recognized Bible story in popular culture. And arguably the most well-known chapter in the Bible is Psalm 23, written by David.

> "*Even those quickly dismissive of the Bible cannot deny that David is among the most famous names in world literature. Were David nothing but a myth, his story would still be the stuff of the greatest of legends. Giant slayer, warrior, outlaw, mercenary, lover, poet, musician, and sometimes prophet, David is great by any measure. Sculpted, painted, debated, denounced, and denied, David is the greatest of all Israel's rulers. One cannot fully understand the history of Israel—nor have a true sense of the Bible as a whole story—without David.*
>
> *Still, some might be hesitant to utter the phrase 'David the Great,' and understandably so. For every Goliath in the life of David, there is a Bathsheba around the corner. For every soul to whom he showed compassion, there were a hundred whom he was personally responsible for slaughtering. He had many wives, yet his palace was also filled with concubines. He had a different woman for every night of the week. His father-in-law hated him, and at least one of his wives despised and betrayed him. One of his sons led a revolution against David and would have executed him had loyal souls not intervened. David caused a devastating plague, and like a Mafia don, ordered the execution of his enemies while on his deathbed.*"[2]

Who does that? And in the Bible, nonetheless. You should read your Bible more, man.

"Yet he was also a Spirit-sensitive poet whose words have comforted millions worldwide in two major religions for 3000 years. Not least of all, David was a man of passionate loyalty, great faith, and national vision. The name of this ancient Jewish king is known where the Bible is not even read or believed."[3]

We discover another side of the man's makeup—lustfulness as a husband, weakness as a father, and partiality as a leader. As author Mark Rutland says, "We need to de-comic-book David and tell the real story.

The real David steals the pretty girl from their husband. The real David makes a mess of his family. The real David breaks the laws of both God and man…He was a complex man, perhaps one of the most complicated and conflicted leaders of all time…We may be shocked by his sins, but we are also inspired by his victories and moved by his intimacy with the God of Abraham."[4]

So, why David? And what does he have to do with the life of a business traveler? Plenty.

- David was a no-name.
- David had a ton of downtime.
- David had a horrible boss.
- David was a leader.
- David was overlooked, disrespected, and dealt with tragedy.
- David was accused of things he didn't do.
- David was guilty of things he definitely *did* do—and paid dearly for it.
- David was tempted in ways we can relate to on the road.
- David was an absentee father.
- David cared about his legacy.

(Need I go on?)

On top of this, trauma and drama marked David's life. Just to mention a few:

- Overlooked by his father.
- Despised by his older brothers.
- Saul tried to kill David.
- Never given the promised financial reward or removal of taxes for his family after killing Goliath.
- Micah (his first wife) was given to someone else after David had to escape.

- David led the armies of Israel into battle and then was pursued by those same armies.
- David defeated the Philistines but then was forced to hide among them to escape Saul's sword.
- David's mighty men wanted to kill him after their town of Ziklag was pillaged and their families were taken captive.
- His best friend, Jonathan, was killed in war.
- His own son Absalom revolted and attempted to take the kingdom.[5]

"No one ever takes it too hard on David. It's probably because he's not much different than us. We see ourselves in his story. There's just something about David; he's a mirror for the world and a reflection of every human heart."[6]

It would be easy to yell at David as you read his story, like he was a clueless character in a horror movie who should avoid the obvious dangers ahead. The dichotomy is this: what we hate in David is what often destroys us, and what we love in David, we want to become.

The life of David offers so many practical lessons for those of us on the road.

He's the only one in all of Scripture to be called "a man after God's own heart." Think about that statement. It isn't "self-proclaimed" like an athlete these days shamelessly self-promoting on social media. God gave him this ultimate descriptive title—even after all David did and failed to do.

(Note: even though our focus is specifically on the life of David, there are numerous characters that come in-and-out of this story. As a result, I included a Cast of Characters resource at the end of the book that I suggest you leverage as a quick reference and further understanding of their specific placement in the life of King David.)

We're going to look at six specific seasons of David's life and apply them to life on the road as a business traveler. This book will follow the stages of David, not necessarily chronologically, but thematically.

1. **David as a No-Name**: We all start out as a no-name, and it happens again every time we change companies. But God uses this time to prepare us in amazing ways so that we can grow and serve others for the rest of our lives.

2. **David as a Warrior**: From his rise to fame by killing Goliath to his developing leadership in King Saul's army, David handles fame in amazing ways—then is tragically disowned and disappears.

3. **David as a Loner**: This is a confusing time in David's life as a fugitive where he questions yet learns to rely on God. As a result, many Psalms are written. This season prepares David to lead.

4. **David as a Leader**: We see many sides of David's leadership during this season, which begins slowly. Here, he often excels but also learns some very difficult lessons that affect those he leads.

5. **David as a Family man**: This, by far, is the darkest season of David's life and paints our hero in a completely different light. Yet, there is so much to learn from his many failures with his closest relationships.

6. **David as a Legacy**: David's ending looks nothing like his humble beginnings. Amazingly, even with all his failures, the man after God's own heart is still in him, and he hands off his kingdom properly.

There are 30 chapters in this book, designed to be read in about ten minutes or less *and intended to be read only while on the road*. If you have a three-day road trip, put your bookmark in at the end of the trip and begin reading day four on your next day on the road.

Each chapter has four parts:

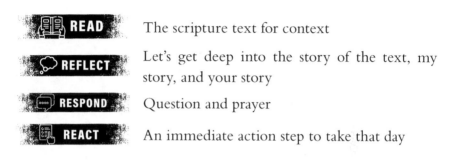

READ	The scripture text for context
REFLECT	Let's get deep into the story of the text, my story, and your story
RESPOND	Question and prayer
REACT	An immediate action step to take that day

God would love nothing more than to change our mindsets about the limits of the road and what it can't give to you. Instead, He wants to teach you to leverage the road and what it *can* give you: a daily opportunity to grow your faith.

Join me on this journey to carve out ten minutes a day to focus on you as a spiritual road warrior, one who is working to become a road warrior after God's own heart.

SEASON ONE
David as a No-Name

1.1 RUNT

Lowest Man on the Totem Pole

Jesse presented his seven sons to Samuel. Samuel was blunt with Jesse, "God hasn't chosen any of these." Then he asked Jesse, "Is this it? Are there no more sons?"

"Well, yes, there's the runt. But he's out tending sheep" (1 Samuel 16:10-11a MSG).

I've been a no-name with a no-name job in a no-name company.

I've been a no-name with a named job in a no-name company.

I've been a no-name with a named job in a named company.

At some point in our lives, we've all felt the obscurity of nobody knowing who we are. It may happen when you join a new company or when you've changed companies and started all over. It might be where you are at this very moment—thinking you would be somebody after all these years, but you feel like a no-name. The runt.

Like the term "no-name" needs to be defined, a quick search of the online dictionary confirms the obvious: *Lacking a recognizable name, identity, or reputation; not noteworthy. A person who is unwanted, unrecognized, anonymous, or not accepted.*

My first memory of this reality was getting dropped off at Liberty University at the beginning of my freshman year of college. I grew up with a well-known father. He was known nationally, and it meant something to be a Buckley. Growing up, I felt the weight of our name…until I went to college, where the Buckley name carried no weight and meant nothing to everyone. I was a no-name.

This was a blessing and curse, something that has continued throughout my life as a pursuit to "be known" and make my own name. It created a self-reliance in me that caused me more pain than good over the years.

I've also felt it decades later when I assumed that I would be at a better place in my life, more known professionally, and further ahead financially. But here I am, still feeling like the runt in too many ways.

> *Whether you are young in business, new to a different company, or still not really known in your company years later, we all find ourselves as a no-name at some point. And we stop our focus there, thinking it's just an unavoidable and unpleasant season.*

But what if there were a different way of looking at this time? What if there were a different level of work that needed to happen during this no-name time? What if we allowed God to do something in us and through us during these frustrating and seemingly meaningless times?

The first time we read about David in the book of 1 Samuel, he's not even on the scene. The first mention of David is his absence. His family is told to go and get him—the youngest, the baby, the no-name—from the field, where he's doing a job that nobody wants to do and literally stinks. It's the job reserved for the runt of the family who was not yet capable of much else.

"The Hebrew word for 'youngest son' is *haqqaton*. It implies more than age; it suggests rank. The haqqaton was more than the youngest brother; he was the *little* brother: the runt, the hobbit, the bay-ay-ay-bee. Sheep-watching fits the family haqqaton. Put the boy where he can't cause trouble. Leave him with wooly heads and open skies. And that's where we find David, in the pasture with the flock."[7]

David enters on the scene in the Bible as the ultimate no-name, the youngest of eight brothers and doing the low-man-on-the-totem-pole job nobody else wants or has to do anymore. David was already thought of as strange, to say the least, and a bragging little liar, regarding his tales of killing lions and bears. I can only imagine their family dinners, where David was easily prodded to tell his latest adventures so his brothers could make fun of him.

"Write any music with your harp today, David? Have any life-or-death encounters today, little bro?" Insert appropriate mocking here.

And his father, Jesse, only played into the taunting and feelings of "less than" and "no-name." He didn't even consider including David in the family when the prophet of God called "the entire family" to sacrifice. Jesse had to be prompted by Samuel to see if there were *any more* sons.

I have five kids, of which four are boys, and their ages range by 12 years. My eldest two can put a beating on the younger two brothers, and it can be relentless. The hard part is that the runt often brings on the brunt of the abuse too easily and plays right into the hands of the oldest brothers. As a father, I can completely see how easy David could've made it too easy for his older brothers. Talk about confirming what you already feel as a no-name.

In David's situation, his three oldest brothers were in Saul's army. They were grown men and soldiers, and I mean certified, real army kind of fighters. No doubt it was easy to pick a fight with the baby of the family.

Back in this time, being the youngest or "the baby" was the exact opposite of today. Nowadays, "the baby can do no wrong." But not during David's era. Being the eldest meant everything, including the coveted birthright.

We'll pick up what happens next in a future chapter, but for now, let's circle back and drill down on his stinky no-name job.

During this time, the job of a shepherd was the kind you settled for. It was dirty and degrading. It's the garbage truck guy or the hotel room service maid who cleans our toilets and makes our beds, the people we so easily overlook. David, the youngest in the family, was handed down this unceremonious task because the youngest was considered the least valuable.

"David was permanently stamped with a low ceiling of worth from his family because this was the value system of his ancient Eastern world; all he could ever amount to was a shepherd and a youngest son."[8]

Maybe you can relate. Perhaps you weren't "highly regarded," to say the least, within your own family. As a result, you seek to be "a name" to replace "no-name" and "somebody" to replace "nobody" in every area of your life—especially on the road. You can appear to have your act together, but you simply feel like just a dressed-up poser most of the time.

Ultimately, David learned, even at a young age and without much guidance, to do his job the best he could as a shepherd. He could have listened to his brothers and remained a no-name. As we'll find out, David's identity and value were found in God, despite his age or his role.

If he only knew what he would ultimately become: a man after God's own heart. (That title, remember, was not self-given. God Himself called David that!)

The same is true of us. Whether you're still a no-name, back to being a no-name, or doing no-name work, God can and wants to use this time in your life to mold you to become a road warrior after God's own heart. These days on the road matter especially to God and, as a result, should matter to you. It's during the no-name days that we have the opportunity to develop outer and inner skills that will serve us moving forward. It's this work nobody sees (except God) that matters most.

So, my prayer for you is that you change your perspective of feeling like a no-name. Instead, allow God to leverage this time in your life to challenge and change you in ways like David that alter the rest of your life.

QUESTION

What could happen if you changed your perspective and let God do something with this stage in your life so that you could become a road warrior after God's own heart?

TODAY'S ROAD PRAYER

God, it's so easy to listen to everyone else's opinion of me.

It's so easy to look at my no-name job and place my value, or lack thereof, in my work only.

It's so easy to be short-sighted and self-focused.

But that's not how You view this season of my life. You see the end of the story but also know what you need to do in and through me right now, even when all I see and feel is uncertainty and irrelevancy.

May I trust You and Your bigger vision for my life.

May I open my heart in the no-name moments to allow You to do the work You want and need to do in me. Change my heart during this time to draw me towards You.

I give you THIS DAY to become a road warrior after Your own heart.

What's the one action item you are going to take as a result of this chapter?

1.2 PRACTICE

Get Those Reps in While Nobody Is Looking

He is a son of Jesse the Bethlehemite who is a skillful musician, a mighty man of valor, a warrior, one prudent in speech, and a handsome man; and the LORD is with him (1 Samuel 16:18 NIV).

But David said to Saul, "Your servant has been keeping his father's sheep. When a lion or a bear came and carried off a sheep from the flock, I went after it, struck it, and rescued the sheep from its mouth. When it turned on me, I seized it by its hair, struck it and killed it" (1 Samuel 17:34–35 NIV).

The no-name periods for athletes or musicians are critical times. It's the practice times when no one is looking or seems to care that make all the difference later on—when the lights are on and everyone is watching. Every professional will tell you that it was during those days that their skills were developed, and their craft began to improve.

You hear the stories of Michael Jordan and Kobe Bryant who were in the gym or the weight room before their opponents or even their teammates are even awake. Nobody knew, but there they were putting in the reps when they were no-names. And they kept perfecting their game, even during the height of their careers. They practiced differently. They leveraged valuable developmental time.

The same is true for David. Working as a shepherd, he had nothing but time and was his own boss. Once he moved the sheep to the next place, he had time to do whatever he wanted.

This was the perfect time to develop two skills that, thousands of years later, we still admire in David:

1. Words: Music/Poetry
2. War: Combat

What a resume! He's a skilled musician, he's a man of valor, he's a warrior, he has control of his tongue, he's handsome, and the Lord is with him.

How impressive that David is in a job that stinks (literally and figuratively), yet he chooses to make the most of it even when he was a no-name. Nobody made him "take that class" nor did he hire a coach or even have a good model or mentor. But this driven youngster leveraged that time that most easily dismiss to develop in ways that would serve him the rest of his life.

In one of my first no-name roles, I remember flying to Minneapolis to do a training with a "corporate slide deck" that was just brutal. Five minutes into a one-hour training, everyone was bored...including me. It was over all our heads, and I was the trainer! I shut my MacBook Air, sat on the desk, paused and asked: "If you let me just ask you a bunch of questions, I'll let you go 30 minutes early. Do we have a deal?"

Everyone perked up and instantly agreed, and the gold I gained in that conversation served me for a decade. I learned what *they* were looking for from a trainer in *their* industry. They talked for the full hour, venting their past frustrations, surprised someone was just willing to ask their opinion.

We know David was a skilled musician because, later in his story, he brings solace to King Saul solely with his musical abilities.

David ultimately wrote at least half of the 150 psalms in the Bible. We don't know exactly when many of them were written, though it's likely some were penned during this time as a shepherd. We do know his skill in music and poetry were part of his early life and must have been developed during his time in this no-name job.

We also know David was skilled in combat. We learn this in the interaction with King Saul when David was thrilled to mention how he is prepared to fight this giant. "But David said to Saul, 'Your servant has been keeping his father's sheep. When a lion or a bear came and carried off a sheep from the flock, I went after it, struck it, and rescued the sheep from its mouth. When it turned on me, I seized it by its hair, struck it, and killed it'" (1 Samuel 17:34–35 NIV).

It's easy to just skim over these two verses, but really absorb what was done. "When a lion or a bear…"

Stop here. He said "when" not "if." And what type of animals? Cute rabbits and foxes? No. Lions and bears. Oh my.

Then he rescued the sheep from its mouth, he had to get close enough to the beast to get the helpless sheep. David didn't have a rifle with a scope that he could use a hundred feet away. He had to physically come and get it. Again, "when" not "if" it turned on him, David seized the lion or bear *by its hair*, struck it, and killed it.

Let me be honest. My first reaction would be to avoid any blood dripping on my new Cole Haan shoes and say, "It's one sharp as a bowling ball sheep, and I have a ton of other ones who are *not* in the mouth of a lion or a bear, so let's keep this in perspective, boss." (Plus, I'd prefer to watch my Chicago Bears beat the Detroit Lions.) Not David.

Combat at that time was nothing like today. Modern warfare is often fought at a distance. In this era, though, it was up close and personal. Their blood was your blood.

David used this no-name time to develop two skills that would bring him fame, allowing his deeds and his words to be studied thousands of years later.

The third, lesser-known skill that was developed was *responsibility*.

As we learned in the last chapter, being a shepherd required a ton of responsibility on any given day. And David was both the boss and the hired help. It was all on him. He was responsible when no one was looking, but so much was on the line.

From this time of development of his skills, David would eventually use his music and poetry, his combat, and his great responsibility in leading the armies of King Saul, his own men, and ultimately the nation of Israel.

Oh, by the way, he did this all as a no-name. He didn't know his future at this point. Even when he was anointed king, he went back to being a no-name as a shepherd to continually develop his skills. Not a personal fan of delayed promotions. Just sayin'.

This may be exactly where you are right now at work. The path of least resistance is to simply exist. Do the bare minimum, stay under the radar, and hope someday it will change.

But what if God strategically put you in this position to learn and develop those outer skills under the radar? What if, in another role or job, you're able to look back and be thankful that you used this no-name time in your career to "shut the laptop, sit on the desk, and ask questions"?

By the way, the intel I gained from that training in Minneapolis has been a template I've used ever since for doing corporate trainings. Every time, it resonates with the audience and exceeds results. It became my secret weapon and will be for years to come. This equation truly works:

> *No-Name Person + No-Name Role x Leveraging the Time = Outer Skill Development*

The key to this simple equation is "Leveraging the Time," which so few of us do on the road. It's a gift that is often hidden on the road. There is a huge difference between wasting valuable no-name time or developing outer skills that can be used in the future.

After killing Goliath and climbing the corporate warrior ladder, did David ever look back to his days as a shepherd, when he worked on his musical ability when only the stars and the sheep heard him? Or where he developed his combat and responsibility skills in his no-name development time?

This no-name time on the road is literally a gift from God. It's your "shepherding time" where you, just like David, can develop your words and your craft as a (road) warrior.

QUESTION

How can you use your time on the road efficiently, especially as a no-name, to develop needed outer skills in your current role?

TODAY'S ROAD PRAYER

God, it's so easy to waste time on the road, especially when nobody is looking and nobody seemingly cares. But You do. You want me to use my time wisely to be the best I can be and develop outer skills You already see in me.

May I leverage every moment to develop the skills that you can use in my life.

I give you THIS DAY to become a road warrior after Your own heart.

Write down three outer skills that you can develop on the road, starting right now, and circle the one that you will focus on first.

1.3 INTERNAL

Inner Training as a No-Name

 **READ**

After removing Saul, he made David their king. God testified concerning him: "I have found David son of Jesse, a man after my own heart; he will do everything I want him to do" (Acts 13:22 NIV).

 **REFLECT**

Bible stories sometimes become so familiar that we miss the true nuance of the details of the story. We're either so familiar with the story that we skim the verses, thinking we already know all there is to know. Or we don't pause long enough to "meditate" and really think through the context or backstory of the character.

David's story is definitely one of those stories. He's called *by God* as a man after His own heart. But when did that actually happen? When did this start?

> *Think about it. When did David get on God's radar that he was a man after God's own heart? Ironically, when David was still young.*

"We would miss the whole meaning of this story if we were to imagine that the first time God had spoken to David's heart was at his public anointing. This was only the outcome of what had taken place in private between David and God long before. David was anointed for his great service and ministry as Israel's king because God, who discerns the hearts of all men, knew that David's heart was different from others. Whenever it was, there had been a moment when God found David, long before Samuel came to Bethlehem and anointed him. There had been a moment of glad response from David to the call of God, a response which renewed his heart and caused him to write, even in his youthful days, such lines as the Shepherd psalm."⁹

As we learned in the last chapter, David used this no-name time to develop his outer skills...and did he ever! The words he wrote into psalms would become the poetry that people turn to in time of need and use to put words to their feelings. And his war skills would go on to not only take on lions and bears, but giants, thousands in battle for Saul, and those pursuing him in the wilderness. Eventually he would lead his own incredible army once he became king.

Yet David could've stopped there, and he would still be impressive. But David went to a deeper level, using this no-name time to develop his *inner* skills as well.

HERE ARE FOUR INNER SKILLS TRAININGS AVAILABLE TO US, ESPECIALLY ON THE ROAD:

1. God trained David in solitude.

Solitude is an attribute of the road. It seems to be either feast (we're always around people) or famine (it's just us and an empty hotel room).

Many of us don't like to be alone and do whatever we can, healthy or not, to avoid that feeling.

There is an important distinction to be established right off the bat: there is a world of difference between *solitude* and *loneliness*, though the two terms are often used interchangeably. Both have to do with the sense of being alone, obviously, but that is about all they have in common.

Loneliness is the negative side of being alone where you feel isolated, like something important is absent from your life.

"Solitude is the state of being alone *without* being lonely. It is a positive and constructive state of engagement with oneself. Solitude is a time that can be used for reflection, inner searching or growth, or enjoyment of some kind."[10]

The road provides a perfect opportunity to turn loneliness into solitude, which can lead to time with God. I believe David, in the no-name days, found solitude as a gift to be developed rather than a punishment of isolation.

"Men and women of God, servant-leaders in the making, are first unknown, unseen, unappreciated, and unapplauded. In the relentless demands of obscurity, character is built."[11]

2. God trained David in silence.

It's one thing to feel alone, but it's a completely different situation to have it *quiet*.

The road is full of noise, especially when we're traveling or entertaining. Then, when we are alone, we immediately default to noise because the solitude is confronting. We feel like we need noise to cut through the silence: the tv, music, the Internet, etc. Something—anything—just not silence.

But it's in the silence that we find our thoughts and often hear that "still small voice" of God, a voice that is easily drowned out by the noise.

David used his alone time of solitude to find silence in his current situation. And I'm confident many of the psalms we read today came from these times.

> *We should learn to leverage the silence the road provides. In doing this, we allow God to develop this inner skill that provides depth to our spiritual lives.*

3. God trained David in trust.

That's a loaded word: trust. It's the "assured reliance on the character, ability, strength, or truth of someone or something; the dependence on something future."[12]

David learned to trust in more than himself and his mad skills. This amazing trust in God was front-and-center when David took on Goliath. His words demonstrated the highest level of trust when his life literally depended on it.

Trusting God in the challenging times is one of my biggest areas of growth as a Christian. I want answers and resolution *now*. But God asks us to "trust in the Lord with *all* of your heart and lean *not* on your own understanding" (Proverbs 3:5 NIV).

4. God trained David in patience.

If there's one thing road warriors lack, it's patience. Yet there are so many opportunities to develop this inner skill on the road: traffic, flight delays, lines to board the plane, rental cars, restaurants, etc.

King Saul was clearly lacking this inner skill and disobeyed God by seeming to trust Him, but then becoming impatient in His timing.

David absolutely had to learn how to be patient and ultimately wait on God. He could trust God, sure, but still had to learn patience. His lessons came in his menial job of watching and caring for sheep, who were never in a hurry. He used this extended time to hone his inner skills and become a man after God's own heart.

You see, God is seldom early but never late. He doesn't run on our timeframe but on what is necessary to develop us. Oftentimes, that just takes time.

Nick Herman lived hundreds of years ago in France. After his time in the army, he then served high government officials and was introduced to all that life potentially had to offer. However, he found it lacking and not at all what he had thought it would be. Eventually, he found Christ and on the advice of his brother, he sought a job in ministry. Nick showed up at a monastery looking for a job and to his shock, they offered him a job on the spot...as a dishwasher. Talk about a no-name job and a boring, seemingly non-influential role.

He had a decision to make. He could leave. He could complain. Or he could leverage this no-name time to do "everything to the glory of God." He could choose to use this no-name period as a gift, offering continual prayer to God and enjoying the companionship of God in all his work. And that's what he did.

People far and wide would come to learn of how Nick was practicing the presence of God, using this no-name time to develop the skills of solitude, silence, trust, and patience. Nick Herman is also known as Brother Lawrence, the author of one of the most impactful and influential spiritual books ever written, *The Practice of the Presence of God*.[13]

David learned in the no-name times that God was the source of His strength, and he built his trust in God by seeking God in the solitude and silence. So many times in his journey we read that "David sought the Lord" or "David inquired of the Lord," and time and again, God proved Himself trustworthy.

David would need these four skills of solitude, silence, trust, and patience one day, when he would find himself as a fugitive. He, no doubt, was thankful he had developed these critical inner skills in the no-name days years earlier, as they would serve him well during the dark days he would experience.

You have a gift God is wanting to develop in you on the road through solitude, silence, and trust. It may look like one or more of the following:

- Choosing to be by yourself at least one evening instead of going out to dinner or sitting at the hotel bar to avoid being alone.
- Choosing to turn off the noise when getting ready for your day, or while driving, so you can hear that "still small voice" of God.
- Admitting to God that you're struggling to truly trust Him and naming those areas: "God, I do want to trust, but help me with my mistrust" is a great place to start.

May you leverage this time on the road to develop these critical inner skills. You don't know how long you'll be on the road, so maximize this gift to grow in these areas right now.

QUESTION

What can you do differently to leverage the gift of solitude, silence, and trust to become a road warrior after God's own heart?

TODAY'S ROAD PRAYER

God, it's so easy to seek to fill the void on the road with people and noise. Maybe I don't even realize that I'm doing it. Maybe, if I'm honest, it's to avoid what the silence will bring to the surface.

But to be molded and used by You, I need to develop the inner skills of solitude, silence, and trust.

Help me today not only to recognize these moments, but to learn to make the most of these gifts that I may grow in You.

I give you THIS DAY to become a road warrior after Your own heart.

Write down three inner skills that you can develop on the road right now, and circle the one that you will focus on first.

1.4 OVERLOOKED

C'mon, Dad, I'm Right Here in Front of You!

Jesse presented his seven sons to Samuel. Samuel was blunt with Jesse, "God hasn't chosen any of these." Then he asked Jesse, "Is this it? Are there no more sons?"

"Well, yes, there's the runt. But he's out tending the sheep" (1 Samuel 16:10-11 MSG).

Try and remember the last time you were talking to someone who really wouldn't give you the time of day. You're there, but you're not. They're scanning the room looking for a better offer, an upgrade. #RightInFrontOfYou

Or here's my favorite. When you walk into a room you weren't suppose to enter and see everyone having a blast, and the fun stops as you enter the room. #SlightlyAwkward

"A 2014 study compared the psychological damage done to employees in the workplace, specifically the difference between *bullying* and *exclusion*. They found that being ignored by co-workers was more harmful to people's emotional well-being than being mistreated by them."[14]

Being overlooked hurts, no matter if we chuck it off as "no big deal" or act all tough about it. Exclusion creates the following emotions:

- Hurt feelings
- Passive-aggressive behavior
- Lack of motivation
- Resentment

Even though we ultimately know David as the famous giant killer, as we've learned by this point, he owned the "No-Name" undisputed title for quite some time. While he probably understood the value of living under the radar, he may have been just as surprised as us at *who* overlooked him.

Quick reminder: the first mention of David is in his absence. Ouch.

Two worlds were going on at the same time. David was doing his thing watching sheep eat. His brothers were on the runway (and not the airport kind,) but one that could change their lives by becoming the next big boss: the king.

Before we unpack this story like a carry-on, let's give a little backstory. The people rejected Samuel the Prophet and asked for a king. God gave them Saul, but later rejected him because he just couldn't get out of his own way. He was really good at playing God instead of obeying God. As a result, God told Samuel to head to Bethlehem (remember that city name?) to anoint the next king.

Samuel rolled into town and shocked the local leadership (the town elders) because the nation's prophet usually only shows up when bad news is about to happen. In fact, they asked "Do you come in peace?" (Side note: If I were Samuel, I would've totally messed with the town elders. I know, right?)

The very act Samuel was to perform was treason, so God gave Samuel a cover story so as not to make King Saul suspicious. God had Samuel sacrifice a burnt offering and respectfully invite the town elders to crash the party. Samuel is told by God that He will show him what to do and who God wants him to anoint.

Samuel came to Jesse's house and began with the eldest brother, Eliab, who was tall (possibly dark?) and handsome and in King Saul's army. Samuel thought, "This is easy, and I can catch an early flight home." (Slight paraphrase.) In fact, God said, "Do not consider his appearance or his height, for I have rejected him." Samuel was enamored by the externals, like most of sadly are, too.

Later in the story, the true heart of Eliab comes out and, in the words of my little guy, "that no good." Eliab was critical and condescending. He was the "that guy" you avoid on a plane. (You know, the guy on his phone all the way down the jetway, while the flight attendant gives her captivating safety speech. You're rude, dude, and not *that* important.)

"When we read about each of David's brothers prancing in front of Samuel the Prophet, it's easy to laugh at them. I'm sure they were strutting as proudly as possible. I would've gotten a kick out of seeing them booted off stage. But...I'm no better than they were. My ego always wants more ego. I'm the king of my own tiny (road) empire."[15]

"For him [David], it was just like any other morning. Little did he know that his life would never be the same again—or that, beginning that very day, he was destined for the throne of Israel...God has some extremely exciting things in mind for His children. For some it may happen tomorrow. For some it may happen next month or next year or five years down the road. We don't know when. For some...it could happen today."[16]

"Scripture dedicates sixty-six chapters to his story, more than anyone else in the Bible outside of Jesus. The New Testament mentions his name fifty-nine times. He inhabits the world's most famous city, Jerusalem. The Son of God will be called the Son of David. The greatest psalms will flow from his pen. We'll call him king, warrior, minstrel, and giant killer. But today he's not even included in the family meeting; he's just a forgotten, uncredentialed kid, performing a menial task in a map-dot town."[17]

"It's highly significant to me that Jesse didn't even have his youngest son in the room. David's dad didn't even take him to the tryout. Talk about a father wound!"[18]

In the verses for today, notice Jesse didn't even ask if he should get his youngest son since Samuel the Prophet had called him out. More proof of how David's dad really felt about him.

"It's remarkable, isn't it, how Jesse reveals two very common mistakes parents make. Number one, he didn't have an equal appreciation for all his children. And number two, he failed to cultivate a mutual self-respect among them. Jesse saw his youngest as nothing more than the one who tended the sheep" (a.k.a. their Fam no-name).[19]

And this is the issue. Being overlooked.

David didn't know it until Samuel the Prophet exposed his father by asking if "all the requested sons were in attendance."

I find Jesse's oversight slighting concerning. Samuel, *The* Prophet comes to your small town and into your house to see all your sons, and you give him 7/8th of the results.

I truly wonder how Jesse justified his slighting…I mean, "decision."

And I also wonder how David felt the moment he walked into the party. You know, the party where *everyone else* is in attendance *except* you (been there and awkward for all involved).

I know how I would've reacted. Outwardly thrilled to be there, cracking a joke, "Sorry I'm late. I hit sheep traffic. It was baahhd." Yet inwardly steaming like in a hot sauna at a nice hotel.

We can only wonder how David felt in the moment, because we've all been there.

Overlooked.

"David was Israel's greatest king. Jesus will sit upon the throne *of David*, son of Jesse—not Abraham's or Elijah's throne, yet Jesse didn't perceive it. We may have to live beyond our father's opinion of our life."[20]

MAYBE JESSE SYMBOLIZES SOMEONE ELSE FOR YOU:

1. Your boss:

No matter how hard you work or do what you're told, the promotion, the bonus, the recognition just always seems to allude you for someone else. Over and over and over.

2. Coworkers:

You try and really try, but you just don't fit in. They don't dislike you, but they don't *really* like you.

3. Client/Customers:

You do just as much as "the other guy/girl" as the competitor and even more, yet they get the deal…and they get asked to attend the "can't miss" event of the year. Or maybe you invite and invite people out only to be politely declined.

4. Family:

You're still overlooked after all these years. No matter how much you've changed, no matter how you've grown, you'll always be overlooked.

5. Friends:

You thought you were closer friends then you were, but you see the pictures all over social media at the party everyone went to and had an absolute blast…excet you.

> *Being overlooked happens often if we really admit it, especially on the road. And the result on the road is even more painful: being lonely.*

"Later, when the question of fathers and sons plays an enormous role in David's life, our minds naturally turn back to this first moment, when his father scarcely even thought of him. David was absent; not present in the scene, or in his father's mind. It took Samuel's question to bring him forth. The man who grows unseen by his father will struggle all his life with children."[21]

I had a good father, but he still left me with some major wounds that took counseling to fully uncover and eventually heal.

The scary question is: what wounds given to me *by* my father am I passing on to my own children *as* a father? This really concerns me, and I hope it does to you, especially as a road warrior.

There were inner qualities in David that needed to be developed, and this could only happen in the no-name season when the lights were off and the stage was empty.

The challenge with the no-name season is that we don't necessarily know when this season will end, and if and when God will ever use these newly developed skills in any way that really matters.

AND IT'S DURING THESE DIFFICULT, NEVER-ENDING SEASONS WE NEED TO REMEMBER...

- **God sees**: When we think no one is looking, He sees the injustice of being overlooked.
- **God cares**: He knows those raw emotions you feel from being overlooked, and He experienced them Himself on earth.
- **God responds**: He's waiting for us to come to Him so He can affirm our identity in only Him.

If you're a believer, God's response should be the only one that matters. But that response takes spiritual maturity to truly believe that God sees and cares about you on the road.

"God saw a teenage boy serving him in the backwoods of Bethlehem, at the intersection of boredom and anonymity, and through the voice of a brother, 'David! Come in. Someone wants to see you.' Human eyes saw a gangly teenager enter the house, smelling like sheep and looking like he needed a bath. Yet, the Lord said, 'Arise, anoint him; for this is the one!'"[22]

QUESTION

What wounds from your past are affecting your present, and ultimately your future?

TODAY'S ROAD PRAYER

God, I can be like David who is too often overlooked, and it hurts more than I admit. I don't always respond the right way: Your way.

But I can also be Jesse on any given day, who overlooks those around me on the road. And some days I can be both David and Jesse on the same day. God help me.

May I remember how it feels to be overlooked and love others as You love them.

I give you THIS DAY to become a road warrior after Your own heart.

Write down the ways you feel overlooked and who caused those feelings.

1.5 REVEAL

Whose Opinion Really Matters

But the Lord said to Samuel, "Do not consider his appearance or his height, for I have rejected him. The Lord does not look at the things people look at. People look at the outward appearance, but the Lord looks at the heart."

Then the Lord said, "Rise and anoint him; this is the one." So Samuel took the horn of oil and anointed him in the presence of his brothers, and from that day on the Spirit of the Lord came powerfully upon David (1 Samuel 16:7, 12-13 NIV).

Have you ever paused and thought about what went through young David's mind as he was summoned in the middle of his shepherd shift to come back to the house? I can only imagine David entering, smelling and looking like you know what to his entire family. At the house was an old guy named Samuel, who David has never met, and the town elders who crashed the party (probably for the food.)

Remember, there was just a *Project Runway* episode for all his brothers that took place before he even entered the room. They've been rejected, so they were more than ready for little bro to enter the room. No doubt they were preparing their jabs for dinner that evening.

So back at the scene of the crime, every eye was on David (and every nose was smelling where he just came from.) His brothers were piling on more disgust for the runt, Dad was possibly feeling a little guilty for not including him, and Samuel was wondering "if this is 'The Chosen One,' then why was he not even included in the first place!?"

David had to be thinking, "Am I in trouble?" And the looks of disdain shot at him from his seven older brothers only confirmed his fears.

But why would his brothers respond that way? It was all about appearance for these boys. How did they size up to everyone else?

Even Samuel the Prophet made a selection based solely on appearance and had to be corrected by God to "*not* look at the appearance." Everyone missed on this one.

Except God.

Appearance is everything these days. "Make a great first impression" or "The first impression is a lasting impression." It's drilled into our heads, especially as business travelers.

I am so guilty of both being attracted to the appearance of someone *and* of judging someone based on their appearance.

I feel so surface, so shallow when I "size someone up" based only on their appearance. But I do. Every. Single. Trip. God, help me.

> *If I could change one thing about my response to people, that would be the thing I'd change: I would like to see people not by face but by heart. Too many times I guessed or judged someone, only to later discover their authenticity and depth.*

"God looked into the heart of David and saw a boy who was neither attached to nor corrupted by the life of appearances. He would not rise and fall on the tide of opinion and prestige. He truly lived from his heart. God looks for those who know they are nothing so that He can do something. God wants to do a work through us, but He will not force His own way into someone whose cup is already filled with himself. It starts with nothing; we're nobodies. It's not easy. It requires a heart-ripping humility that most of us can't bear. It requires knowing that every good thing we do comes from the Very Greatest."[23]

I want to cheer for the anointing of David since it gives a guy like me hope.

Back to the story. David came in, and Samuel saw him after seven very good candidates, or so it seemed by their appearance.

Samuel ignores any opinions or input from other. He only listened to one Voice.

"This is the one."

I love what the scripture says, "So Samuel took the horn of oil and anointed him *in the presence of his brothers,* and from that day on the Spirit of the Lord came powerfully upon David" (1 Samuel 16:13 NIV).

I don't think it was by chance that it was "in the presence of his brothers." Soak that in, No-Name.

And what happens next? It ends with "from that day on the Spirit of the Lord came powerfully upon David."

Did the appearance-driven sons get any of that?

And not only did David receive the Spirit of the Lord but it came *powerfully* upon him. That should give us chills if we truly grasp what just happened.

> *David walks in as a no-name who developed his outer and inner skills during this season, and he is rewarded with the powerful Spirit of the Lord because he was a man after God's own heart.*

As we wrap up the No-Name phase of David's story, think about how challenging David's early life is. Sure, he was marked by God to do great things for Him in his lifetime. But being "set apart" apparently doesn't always mean being used immediately. Between the time of his anointing the moment he is crowned publicly, he endures decades of waiting, running, violence, deception...and more waiting.

"Being a man after God's own heart means living life open and submitted to God's will *and timing*. It means telling Him, 'I'm Yours, and I will trust in You no matter what.'"[24]

God's choice of a road warrior after His own heart is conditional upon your heart response, not a head response. "Is your heart resting upon Jesus? Do you have a believing heart? Does it meditate upon God's word and find comfort in the scriptures? Does your heart desire and seek after holiness? Is it a grateful and humble heart? Is it eternally fixed upon God, or is it a fickle heart, flirting with the things of this world?"[25]

I truly want that kind of heart, at least most days on the road. It's a constant and important struggle, but am I willing to work on the heart as much or more than the appearance? Do I spend as much time with God as I do in the hotel fitness center, the shower, and the mirror in the morning? Clean before God *and* clean before man?

I'm both the judge and the jury. I so easily can be Samuel and only look at the outward appearance. I judge how someone carries themselves. How they look. How they dress. What's their computer, workbag, carry-on. Ugh. I make myself sick just thinking how quickly and easily I size someone up...then down.

But then I sit next to a no-name and am internally (and sometimes externally, by my visual reaction) disappointed that I'm not sitting next to "that guy" or "that girl." Then, more often than not, I'll be blown away by how amazing this person is right next to me once they tell me their story.

We can be shallow and corrupt judges and juries by not looking at all (or sometimes any) of the facts.

I so easily can be Jesse, leaving people out just because they *seemingly* don't make the cut, impressed with everyone else yet excluding those closest to me. I too often miss the gift right before my very eyes, when my eyes are what deceive me the most.

But I've also been overlooked many times and so quickly and easily forget how that feels.

Oh, for the ability to see beyond the obvious. To see beyond the first impression, the bad track record. To see beyond someone's age, or the level of intelligence. To see worth and value down deep inside that God puts on them.

You may be overlooked because people naturally see only the outward appearance. They get stuck on that blasted first impression. Others may only really care about what you can produce or what you can do for me. And looking on the outward is easier; seeing the inward (the heart) takes time, effort, and vulnerability that many simply don't want to spend.

And what about me? How much do I really care to get to know the people with whom I come into contact on the road? Am I willing to take the time and put in the effort? Am I willing to see them through God's eyes, and not just the means to my end?

If we want to improve in this area, here's how it starts:

1. **Time with God, especially each day on the road**: Just a few minutes at the start of your day (with a book like this) softens the heart.
2. **Humility**: Realize that you're fighting a societal norm and the natural default to put yourself above others.
3. **Your schedule**: Who will I be in contact with or meet today that may be easy to look at the appearance instead of the heart?
4. **Prayer**: Seek God and ask for a heart like His that sees people beyond the surface.

As we try to change our attitudes and reactions, keep in mind that there will be some people who we've met before. Maybe in the past, we kept it pretty shallow because it's easy to justify that we were "just keeping it professional." But now it's time to get to know their heart.

THE ROAD IS AN INCREDIBLE GIFT THAT ALLOWS YOU TO SEE BEYOND THE SURFACE.

How? Two ways:

1. **Questions**: I'm amazed at how few questions people ask to get to know someone. This is your chance to really learn about someone.
2. **Listen:** Ask…then be quiet! Seriously. Don't interrupt unless you're asking more questions. Let them feel heard. Be the gift they need in someone.

Enter into their lives with the heart of God. Love them with your attention. Look beyond their appearance. Allow them to open their hearts so you can enter in.

May we seek the heart of God and begin to *really* see others all around us on the road:

- At the airport
- On the plane
- In the restaurant
- In the conference room
- Cleaning our hotel room

It's possible, and let's both start today.

QUESTION

Who can you get to know better and find "their heart" instead of "their appearance" *today* so you can be a road warrior after God's own heart?

1. What is their name?
2. When will you see them?
3. What questions can you ask them to get to really know them?

TODAY'S ROAD PRAYER

God, I naturally and selfishly see the appearance of people first. But that is not what You see. May I have Your eyes to see people on the road today, and to see them as *people,* not commodities to advance my own agenda.

May I discover and get to know the overlooked. Prompt me to ask questions, and give me the focus and patience to truly listen.

And may I use this no-name season you have me in to develop what you want to uncover in myself.

I give you THIS DAY to become a road warrior after Your own heart.

Write down the name of one person whom you will intentionally seek their heart as you seek the heart of God.

SEASON TWO

David as a Warrior

DAVID AS A WARRIOR

2.1 MANAGEMENT

Dealing with the Ultimate Bad Boss

David came to Saul and entered into his service. Saul liked him very much, and David became one of his armor-bearers. Then he sent word to Jesse, saying, "Allow David to remain in my service, for I am pleased with him" (1 Samuel 16:21-22 NIV).

And Saul took him that day and did not let him return to his father's house...So David went wherever Saul sent him.

"Saul has slain his thousands, and David his tens of thousands" (1 Samuel 18:2,5 NIV).

Saul was very angry; this refrain displeased him greatly. "They have credited David with tens of thousands," he thought, "but me with only thousands. What more can he get but the kingdom?" And Saul looked at David with suspicion from that day on. Saul was afraid of David because the Lord was with David but had departed from Saul (1 Samuel 18:7-9, 12 KJV).

Now the Spirit of the Lord had departed from Saul, and an evil spirit from the Lord tormented him (1 Samuel 16:14 NIV).

REFLECT

I've had a few good bosses, many okay bosses, and a few really bad bosses in my career.

Forbes Magazine listed traits bad bosses have in common:

- Lack of appreciation
- Takes credit for others work
- Lacks honesty and/or ethical behavior
- Doesn't lead by example
- Little to no self-awareness
- Lacks empathy
- Uses their team as pawns for their own success
- Focuses on blame rather than solutions and support[26]

Can you relate to any or all these traits in your own bad boss experiences?

When I recall the bad bosses I've dealt with through the years, I could tell you stories for hours. I'm confident you could match or beat me with stories of your own (like any good road warrior can, right?)

But my assumption is that we've never had a bad boss anywhere close to David's worst boss: King Saul.

Let's review where David is in his journey. He went from shepherd and runt to anointed by Samuel the Prophet, all while his father overlooked him and all his brothers looked down on him.

When we get a promotion at work, it's usually a quick transition. A matter of days or weeks.

Not for David.

After his anointing, he's *still* a no-name and goes right back to being a shepherd. Huh? In fact, it's unclear whether David knew for sure that he was anointed *as the next king*. The scriptures aren't crystal clear on this detail. David knew he was anointed (and had some seriously oily hair that day to prove it!) and the spirit of God came upon him powerfully. However, he didn't pack his carry-on and get in an Uber chariot and head to the palace to try on crowns.

He went back to his normal stinky day job as a shepherd.

Ironically, someone in King Saul's service knew about David and his musical ability. You see, when David was given God's anointing, it was removed from Saul, and a very disturbing verse states that an evil spirit came upon Saul. Talk about one-upping an evil migraine!

Nothing at all was giving King Saul any relief, so he was desperate to try anything. He allowed David to come into his presence to play his music to help Saul relax and sleep.

David didn't know it, but he was getting ready to enter boot camp on the road to becoming a king. It would be a training period that would feel like *Groundhog's Day* with seemingly no end in sight.

"He 'came to Saul and attended him.' When David walked into the king's presence, Saul had no idea who he was, this young man standing in front of him with a musical instrument slung over his shoulder. Saul's successor was standing in front of him, and the king never knew it...David came for one purpose—to minister to the king in his depression."[27]

God had His hand on David, whose music not only would fill the heart of a depressed king overwhelmed by darkness, but also would someday fill His written Word. I often wonder if any of the psalms were written while he was providing the background music for his boss.

Then David was brought in full-time to serve as an intern incognito—a king in the making (without Saul realizing it.) And what happened? David prospered. The Scriptures mention that David prospered four times! Even with a bad boss.

So, here David has his first real boss, one who had some traits that are the demise of many of us if we let them.

FOUR HORRIBLE TRAITS OF DAVID'S BOSS THAT STAND OUT

1. The arrogance of a bad boss

I'm never of fan of an arrogant person, especially not in a boss. Arrogance makes everything always about them, and they rarely notice anyone else.

Later in the story when David steps forward to offer his services to take out Goliath, King Saul didn't even recognize that it was David. You know, the one who God used to calm or remove the evil spirit and allowed you relief and rest! C'mon, man!

Arrogance can easily cause anger in me and is a short ride to resentment, especially if it comes from someone in leadership over me.

2. The jealousy of a bad boss

Someone who is jealous has an unhealthy thirst to see another fail at whatever cost possible, and oh, how King Saul was thirsty.

King Saul did his best to put a stop to the praises being heaped on his unchosen rising star. How? He would send him into battles with the sole attempt of seeing David fail, at a minimum. If David were killed, even better. The result? More victory and praise for young David.

Your boss may do some horrible things to you, but do they try to physically kill you? I've been there when you feel like they're trying to kill your career, though, or at least dismantle your confidence—all because of their own jealousy issues.

But King Saul's attempts backfired and only amped up "the praises of his people" tenfold.

"They have credited David with tens of thousands," he thought, "but me with only thousands. What more can he get but the kingdom?" (1 Samuel 18:8 NIV).

3. The skepticism of a bad boss

When you have a skeptical boss, they question and doubt everything. It feels like it's all about you, but actually, it's only about them.

Our story tells us that after the praises kept coming to David, Saul did something different from this point:

"And from that time on Saul kept a close eye on David" (1 Samuel 18:9 NIV).

I'm not a fan of micro-managing bosses, especially when I know what I'm doing. It's easy to take their "close eye" on you too seriously, and it's an unhealthy way to work.

This is when your confidence in God should be at the forefront of your mind, knowing God can and wants to use this time to deepen your trust in Him.

4. The insecurity of a bad boss

I've had insecure bosses, and they're unpredictable at best. Everything you do exposes something in them and, instead of maximizing your strengths for the team, they take it personally.

"Saul was afraid of David, because the Lord was with David but had departed from Saul" (1 Samuel 18:12 NIV).

Someone who has "the spirit of the Lord" creates a confidence (not arrogance or pride) because of who is in and guiding them.

The same is true for someone who "lacks the Lord." Their identity is solely found in their role as a boss, which can bring out some pretty nasty junk.

So, what's your boss throwing at you? Trying to sabotage you? Trying to take or keep you down?

I want my bosses to create an environment where I can succeed and they can succeed as well. But...

BAD BOSSES CAN LEAVE YOU LACKING IN FOUR SPECIFIC AREAS:

- **Lack of reason**: Why are they doing or not doing what they're doing? It could be a result of their arrogance.
- **Lack of responsibility**: Why won't they give you what you know you can handle? It could be a result of their skepticism.

- **Lack of recognition**: Would it hurt them to recognize your efforts just once in a while? It could be a result of their jealousy.
- **Lack of resources**: Why can't they give me what I need to just do my job or a good job? It could be a result of their insecurity.

David, amidst all these issues with his boss, never took it personally. He showed back up for work every single time and did his best. As if "the real boss" (God) was watching him. Hmmm.

Ironically, as David was dealing with the ultimate bad boss, he was a boss as well. He led armies and had hundreds of people reporting to him. No doubt he used what was lacking from his bad boss to enable and empower his people.

> *Often, we learn more from bad experiences than good experiences. Through those in authority over us, God may be trying to teach us how to handle even the most challenging situations.*

God may be using your bad boss right now to reveal areas in your own life that need attention. If that's the case, allow God to soften your heart and teach you how to use this season of your life to form you into who He wants you to become, knowing this boss may be only a means to His end.

May this not get lost in dealing with a bad boss: for strategic reasons, "God brought David into the very place He had planned for his destiny. The dream was becoming more real. David was serving in a different role in the king's palace where he would eventually reign. While a shepherd and musician, David was 'rubbing shoulders' with the most important people in Israel. God was initiating David into a very different world that was directly connected to his call, with which he needed to become familiar. As David played his harp each day, he observed what a king did. Our days of training are critical for our success."[28]

QUESTION

How can you respond differently when you deal with a bad boss in light of your desire to be a road warrior after God's own heart?

TODAY'S ROAD PRAYER

God, you often use people in our lives to expose who we are and who you want us to be. And sometimes these people are in leadership over us and do not have our best interest at heart.

May I be grateful for my current boss in areas that are good, knowing it could change at any time for the bad.

May I allow You to use my current boss—both the good and the bad—to grow me in ways that You want to change in my life.

May my eyes be open to You using this person to grow me into a road warrior after Your own heart.

Write down how the negatives with your current boss can ultimately be used by God for the good.

2.2 STONED

Confidence in the Right Place

 READ

Then the Philistine said, "This day I defy the armies of Israel! Give me a man and let us fight each other." On hearing the Philistine's words, Saul and all the Israelites were dismayed and terrified.

For forty days the Philistine came forward every morning and evening and took his stand.

David asked the men standing near him, "What will be done for the man who kills this Philistine and removes this disgrace from Israel? Who is this uncircumcised Philistine that he should defy the armies of the living God? The Lord who rescued me from the paw of the lion and the paw of the bear will rescue me from the hand of this Philistine."

David said to the Philistine, "You come against me with sword and spear and javelin, but I come against you in the name of the Lord Almighty, the God of the armies of Israel, whom you have defied. This day the Lord will deliver you into my hands, and I'll strike you down and cut off your head. This very day I will give the carcasses of the Philistine army to the birds and the wild animals, and the whole world will know that there is a God in Israel. All those gathered here will know that it is not by sword or spear that the Lord saves; for the battle is the Lord's, and he will give all of you into our hands."

As the Philistine moved closer to attack him, David ran quickly toward the battle line to meet him. Reaching into his bag and taking out a stone, he slung it and struck the Philistine on the forehead. The stone sank into his forehead, and he fell face down on the ground.

So David triumphed over the Philistine with a sling and a stone; without a sword in his hand he struck down the Philistine and killed him. David ran and stood over him. He took hold of the Philistine's sword and drew it from the sheath. After he killed him, he cut off his head with the sword" (1 Samuel 17:10,11,16,26,37,45-51 NIV).

David was too young to serve in Saul's army, but the warrior was already deeply embedded inside the boy.

> *The most famous battle described in the Old Testament was not fought between two armies but between two people. It was the battle in the Valley of Elah between David and Goliath.*

Goliath didn't issue this challenge one time and then leave. Not a chance. His challenge went on for forty days. Every morning and every evening for well over a month, he marched out there, flaunting his size and his strength, daring someone to take him on. Goliath means "shouter." Fitting. Goliath is 9 feet 9 inches tall with a size 20-collar, 10 1/2 hat, and he wears 125 pounds of armor.

"How applicable to any 'giant' we encounter! That's the way with the giants of fear and worry, for example. They don't come just once; they come morning and evening, day after day, relentlessly trying to intimidate. They come in the form of a person or a pressure or a worry."[29] Few things are more persistent and intimidating than our fears and our worries...especially when we face them in our own strength.

The sun rose that morning just like any other morning for both David and Goliath. That's the way it often is in life. No warning. But the truth is, that forty-first morning of Goliath's challenge would be the last day of his life—and the first day of David's heroic life. Nobody announced it. No angel blasted a horn from heaven saying, "Goliath, today you're history" or "David, this is your day."

Goliath had now crossed the ravine at the base of the valley and was coming up Israel's side. You see, if you tolerate a Goliath, he'll take over your territory. He'll move into your camp. He'll take your thoughts that normally ought to be on God, and he'll put them on himself. That's why you can't afford to tolerate giants; you kill them.

David's dad pulled him from his no-name job so he could bring some chow to the 'real warriors' in battle. "David, standing there with the groceries, looks up and down the line of battle-hardened soldiers—a fierce bunch to be sure. 'So, which one of you is gonna go kill this guy. This should be awesome. Looks like I arrived at just the right time.'

'Uh, it's kinda lunchtime,' one of the soldiers said.

'My ankle is hurting.'

'I would, but I fought the last champion, and I don't want to be typecast as *that guy*.'

'I don't want to die today.'

At least one of them was honest."[30]

David is shocked at their cowardice and inaction. How can God's army, led by God's king, let this enemy humiliate them like this? How could they just let this barbarian insult their God? Did they not believe that God would give them the victory over these pagans?

Then David asked about the reward. When he heard about the riches and the king's daughter, he doesn't have to be told twice. "What are we waiting for? If none of you soldiers will take on this uncircumcised heathen who dares to defy the army of the living God, then I will."

David changed direction and chose a different approach. He stepped up and convinced Saul. David was around 17, while Saul was almost 60 and had almost 30 years of military experience and leadership. Saul was the prime candidate to fight Goliath. A head taller than everyone else, a warrior, and a king. But he was also self-interested and had given up on asking God for wisdom.

It's amazing to me that Saul would trust Young David with the fate of all of Israel. Maybe he was worn down after 40 days of taunting by the giant of Gath. Maybe he was won over by David's victories as a shepherd. Or maybe God did the convincing and Saul went along with it, not knowing it was God who was leading him in this direction. Whatever the reason, Saul put the entire nation into the hands of a no-name shepherd boy.

I have to give Saul some credit here. He was now banking on this food-running, sheep-herding, harp-playing musician to represent the entire nation of Israel for its very future. But I also question Saul's motives.

Goliath was all about Control—power, threats, and intimidation.

Saul was all about Escape—delay, avoid, blame, daydream, or run.

Also, Saul—and every other soldier in his army—had a very wrong perspective. They only saw the size of the giant. David, on the other hand, only saw the size of His God. In fact, as he approaches Goliath, David actually begins to *mock* him! Imagine this little whelp of a shepherd boy mocking a nine-foot warrior!

I wonder if David looked back at his three older brothers with a smirk that only the baby of the family can confidently pull off, especially knowing what was about to happen.

Now, let's drill down on Goliath's battle approach and David's battle approach; they were as different as the two fighters themselves.

Author Malcolm Gladwell argues that David was the better warrior. He believes David has superior weaponry, was not burdened by the bulky armor or bronze, and was armed with the equivalent of a handgun. A slingshot required and allowed a whole different level of accuracy compared to a sword. It was skillful. It was shaped by long hours of investment and practice in learning where to strike.

Ancient armies had three kinds of warriors. The first was cavalry, armed men on horseback or in chariots. The second was infantry, foot soldiers wearing armor and carrying swords and shields. The third were projectile warriors, or what today would be called artillery: archers and, most important, slingers.

> *"Slings had a leather pouch attached on two sides by a long strand of rope. Slingers would put a rock or a lead ball into the pouch, swing it around in increasingly wider and faster circles, and then release one end of the rope, hurling the rock forward. Slinging took an extraordinary amount of skill and practice. But in experienced hands, the sling was a devastating weapon.*
>
> *Imagine standing in front of a Major League Baseball pitcher as he aims a baseball at your head. That's what facing a slinger was like—only what was being thrown was not a ball of cork and leather, but a solid rock. According to Eitan Herschel, a ballistics expert with the Israeli Defense Forces, an average-sized stone slung by an expert could travel the length of a football field in three seconds flat. At that velocity, it would have the same stopping power as a .45 caliber handgun. Experienced slingers could hit a target 200 yards away…and David was way closer.*
>
> *Slingers were the preferred method of war. And projectile warriors were deadly against infantry, because a big lumbering soldier, weighed down with armor, was a sitting duck for a slinger who was launching projectiles from a hundred yards away. Goliath is heavy infantry. He thinks he's going to be in a duel with another heavy infantryman."*[31]

When Saul tried to dress David in armor and gave him a sword, he was operating under the same assumption. He assumed David was going to fight Goliath hand-to-hand. David, however, had no intention of honoring the rituals of single combat. When he told Saul that he has killed animals, he wasn't bragging about his courage but that he intended to fight Goliath the same way he has learned to fight wild animals—as a projectile warrior.

Goliath taunts and mocks David, and David's response was a confident speech. However, his confidence was not in himself or his abilities, but in God whose name he mentions seven times.

No one else discussed God. David discussed no one else but God. A subplot appears beyond the outer story. More than "David vs Goliath," this was "God-focus vs giant-focus."

"David sees what others don't and refuses to see what others do… he sees the giant, mind you; he just sees God more so."[32]

And David was clear about what he would do to Goliath:

- Strike you down
- Cut your head off
- Give the carcasses of his army to the birds of the air and beasts of the earth

And David's confidence in God was expressed:

- I come against you in the name of the Lord Almighty, the God of the armies of Israel (whom you have defiled)
- This day the Lord will hand you over to me
- And the whole world will know that there is a God in Israel
- The Lord saves, for the battle is the Lord's
- He will give all of you into our hands (David was speaking to all of the Philistines at this point)

"In one afternoon, David took off the head of a giant and gained the admiration of a nation. The fateful collision of two kings, David and Saul, was now inevitable."[33]

> *David took on his biggest giant with his full confidence in God since he was a warrior after His own heart.*

TWO CLOSING QUESTIONS

1. Who or what are the giants in your life right now?
2. Where is your confidence?

TODAY'S ROAD PRAYER

God, I'm amazed at David's confidence in You when facing his giant. Yet I'm also embarrassed and a little ashamed that my confidence is more like the scared army or the already-defeated Saul.

May I not be like those who never even mention You when facing a challenge; instead, help me to be like David, who only talked about You and found his ultimate confidence in You.

God, I admit I see my giants before I see You, but I want that to change right here, right now.

I give you THIS DAY to become a road warrior after Your own heart.

Write down the biggest giant you're facing in your life right now, and be honest if your confidence is more in God or yourself.

2.3 POPULARITY

The Challenge of Success

So David went out wherever Saul sent him, and prospered; and Saul set him over the men of war. And it was pleasing in the sight of all the people and also in the sight of Saul's servants.

So he sent David away from him and gave him command over a thousand men, and David led the troops in their campaigns. In everything he did he had great success, because the Lord was with him. All Israel and Judah loved David, because he led them in their campaigns. The Philistine commanders continued to go out to battle, and as often as they did, David met with more success than the rest of Saul's officers, and his name became well known (1 Samuel 18: 5,13,14,16, 30 NASB).

Success.

We all long for it. Dream of it. Plan for it. Sacrifice for it. As a kid, it may be hitting the game-winning shot or home run. In business, it's landing the ideal job and climbing the corporate ladder...and getting to skip ladder rungs. #DoubleBonus

David moved up the ranks from just a musician to one of Saul's armor bearers, then to being groomed as a warrior. He started as a no-name, but like any talented athlete or business prodigy, he ultimately got his chance. David just jumped on the scene like Buster Douglas beating Mike Tyson. Nobody saw it coming—except David, who put his confidence in God.

As a result, David gained popularity. He became a national hero. The people began to sing his praises. "Saul made good on his promise to enrich the man who killed Goliath. David became a permanent part of the king's court. David became an overnight celebrity. Very few people would take all that in stride, but David did. He knew how to live with success without having it affect him. It's a rare person who can do that…especially if he is young and has never lived his life before the public."[34]

How you're viewed when you climb the corporate ladder matters to others, especially to God. I know too many people for whom success was just too much for them. It changed them and not for the better. When they no longer need you or have that elusive title of influence, things can change.

"Despite his youth and inexperience, David knew how to conduct himself with everyone. The servants liked him. The troops followed him. And even Saul, when he was not in the grip of his evil spirit, respected him."[35]

Here is the champion of champions, the slayer of the giant, and he went wherever Saul sent him. He was in loyal submission to his king. He served as sort of an intern incognito—a king in the making (without Saul's realizing it.) And what happened? He prospered. Four times in the same chapter we read that David prospered, or that he behaved himself wisely. What a man. He simply did what God led him to do. He submitted to authority, and God lifted him up above his peers.

"Saul didn't know what we know all these years later: David was simply a magnet for the supernatural. Music, lions, bears, Goliath… God was steering David through it all, including the battles Saul intended to be the death of David. In fact, not only was David surviving it all, but with each victory, David increased both his following and his fame. Everyone wanted to stand with the kid who always won."[36]

"David experienced numerous shifts at personal and professional levels during this season of his life. He was enlisted in the King's service. Then he married the king's daughter. He was now active in the palace with the 'First Family,' living in close quarters with the king. He shifted from eating with his father to eating at the king's table. He was no longer watching sheep, but leading armies. Even so, David was not prideful, nor apologetic. He fully embraced these shifts. This is not as easy as it seems."[37]

Through the years, I created a unique expertise of helping global companies to become an American brand. I was the brand evangelist, the front man, and the face of the company in America. Each time I got a little bit better and gained more connections, the company did even better.

But my success was misleading. After a year or two with each company, with me putting the global brand on the U.S. map, they soon forgot how this happened and tried to quantify everything. And this magic bunny was either let go or the contract ended sooner than expected. Poof. Again.

It was frustrating, confusing, and discouraging. Most never realized the amount of effort and secret sauce that went into what I did for a company.

Not David. He succeeded big and everyone noticed. Everyone knew he was not just the new guy but "the guy" everywhere he went.

I'm not sure if you've ever felt that way, but success has its challenges as well.

FOUR CHALLENGES OF SUCCESS:

1. Pride: I did it alone

When you start to get noticed and climb the ladder, it's easy to think you did it all on your own. Pride seeps in, and you so easily forget about everyone else that helped you get to where you are. Sadly, the pride guy is always the last one to know, and God loves us too much to let us stay in this place.

2. Greed: I want more

Once we get a taste of success, it's so easy to want more and more. It can become our sole obsession, even at the expense of other people. We go from helping others to *using* others. Success is a breeding ground for greed, but there's always a cost we may not be willing to pay.

3. Contentment: I did enough

At the top, it's also easy to get lazy. We rest on our past successes and just coast, or we leverage the success of those around us for our own credit. When we get content, we fall from the top. David's contentment led to lust, adultery, lying, murder, and more lying to cover it up.

4. Unteachable: I know it all

Success often increases the size of the head but not the brain. We may not say it, but we sure act like we know it all. God has a way of humbling us when we get to the place of being unteachable, and it's often a painful place. Those who stop learning easily get passed by.

David at this stage in his life handles success in an amazing way. How? He was grounded in his identity in God. David still intimately felt God's anointing, and it was evident. He continued to find his confidence in God.

I believe David learned how to handle success consistently by leveraging one word, a word we like *done to us* rather than have to do to others. It's an action that becomes rarer the higher the success.

Serve.

David learned to serve at an early age:

- He served his father by bringing food to his brothers.
- He served while still a shepherd, even after his anointing.
- He served King Saul, playing music and bearing his armor.
- He even served the army of misfits that he would lead in the wilderness.

And he kept that attitude even as he became more successful.

It's hard to be proud when you're carrying a towel to serve others. My father was a great example of this for me. He was nationally known but would be the first one to pick up the towel to help others and serve with the servers. Often at an event where he was speaking, you would find him setting tables and handing out food and drinks to the very people he would soon be speaking to. It spoke volumes far bigger than words, this willingness to serve and not just sit back and be served due to his position and success.

One more point on success. When success becomes elusive or humbles you, who do you turn to in those difficult moments? David constantly brought his concerns to God through the laments in Psalms. And not surprising, many of those laments ended with "but I will put my trust in You, God."

How are you handling your success right now? Feeling higher levels of pride, greed, or contentment? Being more unteachable than you should be? How different would your answer be from the one your coworkers or your spouse might give about you?

May we learn from the life of David how to handle success. May we be willing to make the necessary changes right now, voluntarily, before God chooses to break our attachment to success in ways that may be very painful.

QUESTION

Which one of the four challenges of success are you struggling with the most right now?

TODAY'S ROAD PRAYER

God, I love the feeling of being successful, sometimes too much. I find how quickly I forget You the more successful I become. I credit *me* too much and don't credit *You* nearly enough.

I realize my success is a result of Your favor, but my identity in You is far more important than my success.

I'm humbled by the example that You were fully God yet, being fully man, chose to serve others as Your default mode.

May I leverage any success I have on the road to serve those around me. Let me show them You by my actions and not just my words.

I give you THIS DAY to serve to become a road warrior after Your own heart.

Write down one way you can serve those around you today in a tangible way while on the road.

2.4 DISCERNMENT

How to Know Which Battle to Fight

And David took his stick in his hand and chose for himself five smooth stones from the brook, and put them in the shepherd's bag which he had, even in his pouch, and his sling in his hand; and he approached the Philistine (1 Samuel 17:40 ESV).

So this is my prayer: that your love will flourish and that you will not only love much but well (Philippians 1:10a MSG).

When you're young, you're looking for a fight—any fight—to prove you're a warrior. You are itching for battle, to show everyone you are worthy and can handle it. You also may be looking for a fight when you change companies or roles and need to prove yourself all over again.

I've witnessed too many road warriors who couldn't tell which battles were worth the fight and which battles to let slide. I've seen others who came on too strong and with such force, all it took was the opponent to move and they found themselves flat on their face.

And David was no different. He was young, full of potential, and working his way out of the no-name phase in his early career.

Knowing what battles are worth the fight and what battles to avoid is critical to your success, no matter what your age or season of your career. This judgment is especially needed, though, when you're on the rise.

There were countless battles that appeared in David's life where he had the choice whether to engage, surrender, or just let them go and let God handle the fight.

But there is one specifically that he picked with a giant.

Back to David's story with Goliath. The Scriptures mentioned David grabbed five stones in preparation for his battle with Goliath. We also know his approach was artillery, not heavy infantry.

So, why did he grab five and not just one? There are theories on why he chose five stones. It seems that there are times when the number five represents humanity, human nature, and the human body; for example, five fingers, five toes, five senses, etc. Some of the church fathers talk about five wounds of Christ. Another theory suggests it was because Goliath had four giant brothers. (Imagine being the runt at only 9 feet tall. C'mon, man!)

Here, David combined his faith in God with a practical mind. "He didn't foolishly say, 'The Lord is going to do it anyway, so I'll just pick up any old jagged rock,' He recognized human responsibility and Divine providence and selected (five) shiny, round stones that would speed straight to the mark."[38]

I can only imagine David finding just the right stones with his heart pumping, knowing this would be the fight of his life. Yet, he also had the peace that passes all understanding because he knew God would ultimately determine the outcome of this iconic battle.

Like David, it's easy to have extra stones ready for others coming after you. Maybe you have a stone for one or more of the following in your life:

FOUR ADDITIONAL STONES

1. The co-worker: David's Brother

When David showed up at the battle, Eliab was definitely looking to pick a fight. He was still hacked by getting shown up and passed over on the day of David's anointing.

"David's oldest brother recognizes his youngest brother's voice and comes storming toward him. 'What are you doing over here you little twerp? Shouldn't you be back home with your sheep and imaginary lions? I know your wicked heart, little brother.'"[39] Any chance Eliab has a bone to pick with little bro after losing the undisputed runway championship of Bethlehem to David?

But here's the point: His co-worker was a distraction.

When I was new to the business travel role, I had two nemeses who did everything they could to not just discourage me but devalue me. Their words were condescending and intentional, and their goal was to intimidate me. Fortunately, my CEO, a strong Christian named Rod, realized it. Rod saw this as a growth opportunity for me. So many times, he pulled me aside and let me know that they were only a distraction to get me focused on what was unimportant. Rod encouraged me to still show Christ in my responses.

Often, God will allow these distractions to test us and grow us, but we need to "discern what is best" and avoid engaging in no-win fights.

2. The boss: King Saul

Little did Saul know but he was grooming his replacement. Saul had so many issues in every part of his life, but God used those issues to prepare David.

Saul threw spears at David. He tried to put David in his own armor to fight a battle which should've been the king's job. Saul and his army chased David like a fugitive. Seems David had ample opportunities to pick a fight with his boss.

But here's the point: His boss was a doubter.

Saul was all about self-preservation and doubted everyone, including himself.

It still amazes me how David chose time and time again, not to pick a fight with King Saul. If anyone deserved to go after this bully, it was David. Was he tempted and came close to swinging? Of course. Yet he respected God's anointed (his boss) and consistently went to God to handle this fight for him.

I had a boss who hired me for my experience but doubted every move I made. Seemingly every sentence started with "Are you sure? Maybe you should just…" Doubting bosses are everywhere. You may not have a choice to move on, but you do have a choice whether or not to engage in that fight.

3. The competitor: Enemies of God's people

David had many a competitor in his time: from his brothers and King Saul to the Philistine people and even his own son Absalom.

There will always be people that are trying to take your company down—or even you personally. Competition is inevitable in business and if focused on too heavily, it can take you off your specific role and mission. They want you to focus on them and not on you.

But here's the point: They are divisive.

Too easily the competitor can pull you off your game and get in your head, and bad things happen, especially when they're not playing fair.

I had one competitor who was good at one thing: playing by their own rules. They would talk poorly about our product, and especially about me personally. It got messy and made it all the way to my CEO overseas. Thankfully, my character passed the test, and the situation only went away. It also allowed me to share my faith of how I was able to handle the situation without fighting back unfairly. I had many a mentor guiding me through this process, and I ultimately trusted God to fight this seemingly un-winnable fight.

The competitor can cause you to try and pick a fight that may not be worth your time and energy.

4. The former you: Your own worst enemy

Sometimes the biggest battle to avoid is between your eyes and in your head. It's the person looking back in the hotel mirror and talking trash, and oh, is he or she good at it!

David, amidst all his battles and success, could conquer thousands but couldn't fight his own lust, which led to adultery and murder. He also was not willing to engage in battle with his family when unthinkable acts were taking place with his own kids. He chose, instead, to be passive and avoid any conflict.

But here's the point: Know Thyself.

Our lives may look as different as first class and the last middle seat in the back of the plane, but we're human like David. We have opportunities to engage in battles we should leave alone, succumb to battles we need to flat out flee, and fail to fight the battles within our own family that need our fight for leadership.

"So often, when facing our own giants, we forget what we ought to remember and we remember what we ought to forget. We remember our defeats and forget our victories. Most of us can recite the failures of our lives in vivid detail, but we're hard-pressed to name the specific remarkable victories God has pulled off in our past."[40]

HOW DO YOU KNOW WHICH BATTLE TO FIGHT?

I've found this three-step strategy especially effective on the road when discerning which battles are worth one of your stones:

- **Pause**: No decision on the road is life-or-death, so a pause is absolutely critical. More times than not, simply *not* reacting has saved me so much regret. It removes the emotion and allows me to think.
- **Pray**: We rarely pause then pray for discernment on the road, but it's one action David did often: inquiring of the Lord. He took the pause to pray and see if the Lord is leading him in a clear direction.

- **Predict**: Where will this battle lead if I choose to engage, or should I let this one go altogether and live to fight another day? Often, if we pause and pray, the clarity to predict the outcome comes very clearly.

Back to the stones, David was prepared by having the five stones. He was ready, but he didn't use them up all at once by picking fights with everyone around him. He demonstrated the verse at the beginning of the chapter: "(Pray) that you will be able to discern what is best."

I often wonder what David did with the remaining four stones. Did he discard them since he didn't need to use them? My assumption is no. I believe he saved them, at least one as a reminder of God's provision for him when facing his giant.

"God doesn't waste victories. When He pulls something off that only He can do, He says to us, 'Now, don't you forget that.'"[41] Use your stone as that needed reminder on the road.

QUESTION

What fight are you engaged in right now that you need to get the stone out of your sling and put it back in your bag?

TODAY'S ROAD PRAYER

God, I'm so used to a machine-gun approach as opposed to choosing one stone at a time. I'm willing to fight anyone who challenges, slights, or offends me.

But this is not Your way. You want me to pause, pray, and predict what You would have me to do.

May I learn to discern which battles to fight and which to let go.

May I learn to seek You more on the road for Your peace that passes all human understanding.

I give you THIS DAY to become a road warrior after Your own heart.

Find a smooth stone today by taking a walk outside. Put the smooth stone somewhere visible for the rest of your trip, and keep it in your work bag as a reminder for future business trips.

2.5 LOYALTY

The Must-Have Friend on the Road

After David had finished talking with Saul, Jonathan became one in spirit with David, and he loved him as himself. From that day Saul kept David with him and did not let him return home to his family. And Jonathan made a covenant with David because he loved him as himself. Jonathan took off the robe he was wearing and gave it to David, along with his tunic, and even his sword, his bow and his belt (1 Samuel 18:1-4 NLT).

Saul told his son Jonathan and all the attendants to kill David. But Jonathan was very fond of David.

Jonathan spoke well of David to Saul his father and said to him, "Let not the king do wrong to his servant David; he has not wronged you, and what he has done has benefited you greatly. He took his life in his hands when he killed the Philistine. The Lord won a great victory for all Israel, and you saw it and were glad. Why then would you do wrong to an innocent man like David by killing him for no reason?" (1 Samuel 19:1, 4-5 NIV).

Jonathan said, "Go in peace! The two of us have vowed friendship in God's name, saying, 'God will be the bond between me and you, and between my children and your children forever!'" (1 Samuel 20:40-42 MSG).

While David was at Horesh in the Desert of Ziph, he learned that Saul had come out to take his life. And Saul's son Jonathan went to David at Horesh and helped him find strength in God (1 Samuel 23:15-16 NCV).

I've had several "good friends" through the years. Many I've lost touch with, and some I'm still in contact with years later.

Then there are the "close friends" who've been through thick-and-thicker with me. They came closer to me during the hardest of times. And when I look back, their proximity and the sacrifice of their presence, not just their words, made all the difference.

We find David at this point in his life on the cusp of falling from the height of his popularity. He is entering the darkest time of his life, as a fugitive, thanks to the worst boss ever.

No doubt he had many a friend due to his fame, which will soon fade. When you're on top, friends are everywhere. But what happens when things get hard and friends get thin?

God gives David a gift that few of us ever really experience in our lifetime: a best friend. A friend that is "closer than a brother" (Proverbs 18:24 NIV).

During these trials and changes, David becomes best friends with Jonathan, the son of King Saul. Really, David? The king's son? But friendship holds no restrictions, even in the most unlikely of circumstances.

The King James Version helps paint a more vivid mental image: "The soul of Jonathan was knit with the soul of David" (1 Samuel 18:1 ASV). The word *knit* literally means "chained."

This was a bond that was deeper than convenience and a few common interests. A friendship this deep has a level of commitment that we all long for at some point in our lives, especially when we're on the road.

JONATHAN PROVES HIS COMMITMENT IN THREE TANGIBLY POWERFUL WAYS:

1. Stands Up

Jonathan shockingly and remarkably stands up for Jonathan to his father who, mind you, is equally king and certified mad (and I don't mean angry).

Jonathan takes his life into his own hands knowing his father is not beyond killing his own son. But Jonathan's commitment to David is stronger than his fear of his father.

It would've been easy for Jonathan to back away from David, to put some distance between himself and the man whom his father made public enemy number one. At some point in all of this, the irony is that Jonathan realized that he would never be the next king, and David had been given the anointing. That alone should have been sufficient reason for Jonathan to help Saul kill David.

But instead, Jonathan defends David in front of Saul. Are you serious, Clark? (Think Cousin Eddie in *Christmas Vacation*.) The Scriptures tell us "Jonathan spoke well of David to Saul his father and said to him, 'Let not the king do wrong to his servant David; he has not wronged you, and what he has done has benefited you greatly'" (1 Samuel 19:4-6 NIV). Boom! Talk about a stand-up guy—and to your dad, of all people! Jonathan, my man. And mad kudos (but not like the dad mad, if you know what I mean.)

He protected David from his father, no matter the cost. He told David, "May the Lord be with you as he used to be with my father" (1 Samuel 20:13 NIV). "Jonathan refused to let his father's madness ruin the best friendship he ever had, and in return, he and David were friends in a way that most of us will never really experience."[42]

Oh, to have a friend, and be a friend, that stands up when it matters the most.

2. Shows Up

Jonathan often comes to David. He shows up in the hardest times in David's life when he needed somebody special, a best friend.

He comes to David in two key moments:

1. David needed proof that King Saul was trying to kill him, and Jonathan verified this.
2. David was in the next phase of his journey and on the run.

When Jonathan goes to David, he doesn't say, "Trust me, I got you." We read in 1 Samuel 23:16 NIV that Jonathan "helped [David] find strength in God." The Hebrew words there are "Jonathan strengthened his hand in God." As David and Jonathan gripped hands, they were first gripped by the very hands of God. Yet as David and Jonathan had to part, God never did.

Jonathan became an accomplice. If he was caught with David, they would've been executed together. Essentially, Jonathan became poison too. To strengthen David, Jonathan had to become weak and guilty by association.

It was risky to stand up and risky to show up in David's life during these volatile times. Most would silently exit stage left and have an alibi as a cover. Not Jonathan.

I went through a very long dark period in my life and one of my biggest losses (among many) was people not showing up. Their absence hurt almost as much as the trial, and it painfully and deeply taught me about the value of friendship. Oh, how a Jonathan in my life could've made a tremendous difference to me during the hard times.

3. Sacrifices Up

Jonathan is in line to be the king, but he's not bound to the crown. He cared first about David's life and future. Jonathan firmly wants David to know, "I'm the heir, but you should be king. I never want this to get between us."

The most famous gifts in the Bible are probably the ones the magi gave to the newborn King of the Jews: gold, frankincense, and myrrh" (Matthew 2:11 NIV). "They held more significance than these scholar-scientists realized. Gold represented Jesus' royalty, frankincense His deity, and myrrh His humanity."[43]

Unlike the magi, Prince Jonathan was not giving a complete stranger such personal and significant gifts. For several years, David had come to his house to sing and play for a father with some serious issues. Jonathan was grateful for David's calming effect on his dad. However, after this faith-empowered victory, Jonathan saw David in new light. He initiated a covenant relationship by giving David his robe, his weapons, and his belt. Let's drill down on the symbolism of these three gifts:

The Robe

Jonathan's robe identified Jonathan as a prince. Wherever he went wearing that robe, everyone knew he was royalty with all the privileges and authority that came with the distinction. By giving David his robe, Jonathan placed on him prince-hood. He no longer considered him a mere shepherd, but royalty. A prince! King James includes "his garments" and NIV "along with his tunic." This was more personal than just his princely robe. He also gave him literally the shirt off his back. It meant he didn't mind if David was mistaken for him, or himself for David.

The Weapons

Giving David his weapons represented a commitment to defend and protect. Jonathan gave David two specific pieces: his sword and his bow. A sword represents strength and resources behind David. The bow symbolized an individual's or nation's power and ability to accomplish the intended purpose. Jonathan's bow represented both. He committed his and all of Israel's power and abilities to support this one who should've been an enemy.

The Belt

In David and Jonathan's day, a belt was far more than a way to hold your pants up. It was an important and functional part of a soldier's uniform, often holding small swords, money, and other valuables. Belts were often symbolic too, with the decorations and design signifying an affiliation, status, or victory in battle.

"When Jonathan gave these gifts to David, David knew Jonathan was giving himself to their relationship. Jonathan could not have given David anything more significant or precious than these three incredible sacrificial gifts. They were cherished for a lifetime as a constant reminder of their precious covenant relationship and a motivation to live up to the symbolism of these gifts."[44]

I find this incredibly ironic. Jonathan gives but doesn't receive anything back. You find no returning David's love. The covenant was based on Jonathan's love, not David's response. What an intimate moment, one that was completely one-sided.

God knew that David needed an intimate friend to walk with him through the valley of death that was ahead of him. They developed their friendship in the good times, which prepared them for the bad times.

We also need that type of friend on the road in the good times, when it feels like we can do no wrong and we are at the top of our game. But we especially need them in the bad times, when it feels like everything we do is wrong and we're sitting on the bench watching the game.

We need this type of friend who stands up, shows up, and sacrifices up for us on the road. It is someone who will bear all, who will accept us no matter what, who will challenge us, and who will bring out the best in us, especially in our road life.

QUESTION

Who is your Jonathan in your life, or who has the potential of becoming this type of friend?

TODAY'S ROAD PRAYER

God, friends on the road are few and far between. I find myself wanting more than mere acquaintances to keep me from being lonely.

But I long for this friend that is closer than a brother. A friend who stands up for me, shows up for me, and sacrifices up for me as I fight the battles the road brings to me on any given day.

May I be that type of friend to others as You bring this type of friend to me.

I give you THIS DAY to become a road warrior after Your own heart.

Write down the close friends in your life and the role they currently or could play in your life on the road.

SEASON THREE
David as a Loner

3.1 CRUTCHES
Removing Your Rough Edges

Saul stormed at Michal: "How could you play tricks on me like this? You sided with my enemy, and now he's gotten away!" Michal said, "He threatened me. He said, 'Help me out of here or I'll kill you.'" David made good his escape and went to Samuel at Ramah and told him everything Saul had done to him. Then he and Samuel withdrew to the privacy of Naioth (1 Samuel 19:17-18 MSG).

David got out of Naioth in Ramah alive and went to Jonathan. "What do I do now? What wrong have I inflicted on your father that makes him so determined to kill me?" But David said, "Your father knows that we are the best of friends. So he says to himself, 'Jonathan must know nothing of this. If he does, he'll side with David.' But it's true—as sure as God lives, and as sure as you're alive before me right now—he's determined to kill me" (1 Samuel 20:1,3 MSG).

That day David fled from Saul and went to Achish king of Gath (1 Samuel 21:10 NIV).

Once the dust settled (literally) for David, the reality of what just happened set in. No doubt there were some dark days, even amidst the heat of the desert sun.

David went from a no-name to "the name" being sung by everyone. Well, everyone except King Saul, the one with the power to change everything. And that he did.

David was surrounded by people whom he led, people who seemingly loved him no matter what. Now that no-matter-what had happened, though, nobody was there. He had to wonder what everyone thought of him now in his absence. The no-name who became "the name" is now a name tied to speculation and suspicion. David was "most wanted" for a completely different reason.

For me, it was the vanishing of a secure job on a great team. My boss and I received the bullet at the same time on the same call, after we had been affirmed over and over that we were completely safe.

Emotions hit me hard. I went from numb to afraid. I lost a high-paying job. We lost insurance. I felt and assumed I'd also lost credibility in the industry.

My support system all around me was gone instantly. I was confused, discouraged, scared, and angry.

How could this happen? What did I do wrong? What could I have done differently?

Then it turned to, *How could God let this happen to us? Why me? Why now?*

I went from feast—where life was great and things just could not be better—to complete famine.

Little did I know how God was going to use this wilderness in my life to form me. But He had to remove crutches in my life in an extreme way to get my attention. God chose the same approach with David.

Let's go back to his story...

David was just instantly put on the run going from the comfort of the palace to the barrenness of the wilderness. And it was here that David had certain crutches in life quickly and brutally ripped from his life.

Did David know these crutches needed to be removed? Unlikely.

Did David know what crutches needed to be removed? Nope.

Did David know how these crutches were going to be removed? Thankfully, no.

But God loves us too much to leave us the same. He cares far more about our character than our comfort. He's in the transformation business, not the convenience business.

Sometimes I wish God would just tell me my future. Then other times, I'm so glad He didn't because I would *not* want to know what was coming, especially if I couldn't change it.

David did not see going from Giant Killer to Cave Dweller in the script. He might have asked for an edit or declined the leading role.

Yet God knew this scene in the story was necessary to continue to make David a man after God's own heart. It's easy to worship God when things are good, but when nobody is singing your praises, what happens then? It's harder to sing God's praises in the dark and with no voice to sing.

God chose to remove certain crutches in David's life that had created a dependence that was good for a time. Now, God needed to do a work in David in a way and a place that would develop him even more.

THE REMOVAL OF FIVE SIGNIFICANT CRUTCHES[45]

Crutch #1: The crutch of a good position

David was brought into the army, and he proved himself a faithful, even heroic soldier. Now, it was all gone in the flash of a spear. Never again would he serve in Saul's army. He went from leader to loner before anyone even knew what happened.

Crutch #2: The crutch of David's wife

David then went to his wife who said she truly loved him. Michal, Saul's daughter, helped David escape from her mad father in one moment of heroism. In the next moment, she betrayed David by lying to Dad to protect herself saying, "David threatened to kill me if I didn't help him." In essence, David's wife deliberately walked away from him.

Crutch #3: The crutch of his mentor, Samuel

Suddenly, David was running through the hills, trying to find some secure place to hide. He logically ran to Samuel the Prophet, who took him to a seemingly secure place so they both wouldn't be found. But someone informed Saul of their location, and David no sooner unpacked his carry-on than he was back on the run. Alone.

Crutch #4: The crutch of his best friend, Jonathan

David found Jonathan and demanded to know why his best friend's dad was trying to kill him when he's done nothing wrong. Jonathan did as much as he can, but David must rely on the gifts and memories from his best friend.

Crutch #5: The crutch of his self-respect

That's the last crutch. In fact, it's the lowest tide of a person's life when you lose belief in yourself. At this stage, you doubt everything and everyone, including God.

But David is at a place where everything is removed from his life. He had a position and lost it. He had a wife and lost her. He had a wise counselor and lost him. He had a best friend and lost him. All that was left was his self-respect, and that was soon gone, too.

David made a couple of unthinkable and uncharacteristically bad choices, which we'll learn about in the next chapter. It's what happens when we get desperate.

ROAD CRUTCHES

The road can very easily create crutches that we depend on, possibly *only* on the road. These dangers become escapes, stress releases, and potentially destructive behaviors that we turn to, maybe too often:

- Drinking
- Pornography
- Risky behavior

I've been that guy, and I've talked to too many road warriors who have created crutches that have brought them serious consequences. Many times, they didn't bring on the pain, but they made the pain worse. Other times, they created the pain and then made it worse through destructive behaviors, all enabled by life on the road.

As believers, God's love is so great he can choose to remove those crutches:

- Being cited with a DUI
- Getting caught with porn
- Losing your job (and that great title)

When I've had consequences from my road crutches, I've had my counselor (who wrote this book's foreword) remind me of this verse: "No discipline seems pleasant at the time but painful. Later, however, it produces a harvest of righteousness and peace for those who have been trained by it" (Hebrews 12:11 NIV). *The Message Bible* puts it this way, "At the time, discipline isn't much fun. It always feels like it's going against the grain. Later, of course, it pays off big-time, for it's the well-trained who find themselves mature in their relationship with God."

I've been the slow learner by not allowing the discipline to teach me. But as I seek to be a road warrior after God's own heart, my spiritual maturity grows along with my relationship with God...and it affects how I respond differently next time.

THREE WARNINGS TO ALL WHO PREFER CRUTCHES

1. Crutches become substitutes for God

If one of my crutches is serving me well, it's all I need. In reality, it has become my idol and a substitute for God. I don't like to admit it, but that's exactly what my crutches become. I turn to them, not God.

2. Crutches keep our focus horizontal

I know if I'm using one of my Road Crutches, I conveniently skip my Bible reading and prayer time. I don't want the guilt and the conviction from the Holy Spirit. How's that for honesty? I will also try to work things out on my own, thinking I know what is best.

3. Crutches offer only temporary relief

The quick hit of that [road] crutch always wears off and often leaves us feeling guilty and always wanting more. This should be an obvious sign you have a [road] crutch and God may be trying to get your attention.

I've learned through many years of doing things the hard way, God is going to get my attention to remove these crutches—with or without my permission.

VOLUNTARY VS. INVOLUNTARY BROKENNESS

Voluntary brokenness is when we willingly soften our hearts to the brokenness process. We listen to the prompting God is giving to us and make the choice to succumb to the brokenness. As God was removing these crutches, David allowed the voluntary brokenness process to continue to mold him into the man after His own heart.

Involuntary brokenness is when we harden our hearts to the brokenness process, and God steps in. Often this means harsh consequences. Circumstances stop us in our tracks and get our attention, sadly, when we have little to no other choice. David would experience involuntary brokenness in the coming years with adultery, deception, and murder in the saga with Bathsheba.[46] (Note:

Your heart can still change at this stage, but the consequences often last for a lifetime.)

My prayer for you as a spiritual road warrior is to allow any crutches that God is trying to remove in your life. I strongly urge you to soften your heart and choose voluntary brokenness to avoid the intervention of involuntary brokenness.

QUESTION

What crutches are you depending on right now on the road that God may want to remove in your road warrior life?

TODAY'S ROAD PRAYER

God, when things get hard, instead of turning to You, I often take over. I want control, sadly thinking I know what is best.

I also want to rely on everything and everyone else *except* You. Lord, have mercy on me, a sinner.

You love me too much to let me stay where and how I am. This process may be painful, and I acknowledge it right now.

May I choose voluntary brokenness in this moment, instead of having You step in to remove crutches so I can find You.

I give you THIS DAY to become a road warrior after Your own heart.

Write down the one crutch that you need to begin to remove today and how you will remove it.

3.2 DECEPTION
Desperate Times and Desperate Measures

David went to Nob, to Ahimelech the priest. Ahimelech trembled when he met him, and asked, "Why are you alone? Why is no one with you?"

David answered Ahimelech the priest, "The king sent me on a mission and said to me, 'No one is to know anything about the mission I am sending you on.' As for my men, I have told them to meet me at a certain place. Now then, what do you have on hand? Give me five loaves of bread, or whatever you can find."

But the priest answered David, "I don't have any ordinary bread on hand; however, there is some consecrated bread here."

Now one of Saul's servants was there that day, detained before the Lord; he was Doeg the Edomite, Saul's chief shepherd. David asked Ahimelech, "Don't you have a spear or a sword here? I haven't brought my sword or any other weapon, because the king's mission was urgent."

The priest replied, "The sword of Goliath the Philistine, whom you killed in the Valley of Elah, is here; it is wrapped in a cloth behind the ephod. If you want it, take it; there is no sword here but that one."

David said, "There is none like it; give it to me."

That day David fled from Saul and went to Achish king of Gath. But the servants of Achish said to him, "Isn't this David, the king of the land? Isn't he the one they sing about in their dances:

'Saul has slain his thousands, and David his tens of thousands?'"

David took these words to heart and was very much afraid of Achish king of Gath. So he pretended to be insane in their presence; and while he was in their hands he acted like a madman, making marks on the doors of the gate and letting saliva run down his beard.

Achish said to his servants, "Look at the man! He is insane! Why bring him to me? Am I so short of madmen that you have to bring this fellow here to carry on like this in front of me? Must this man come into my house?" (1 Samuel 21:1-14 NIV).

It's so easy to trust God when we don't feel we have anything to trust Him with at the moment. It's harder to trust him when the things that we value start to slip away.

And that could be no truer than our choices on the road, during desperate times and through desperate measures.

"The ways of God are most unappealing and they seem the most irrelevant when we're angry, alone, or afraid. We feel compelled to do about anything to make something happen. Things rarely get better but worse. We force things and why? Because when we're angry, alone, and afraid, we often panic."[47]

Do you remember crutch #5 from the last chapter? It was the painful crutch of self-respect. This crutch is unpacked in the two very unusual stories you just read at the beginning of the chapter.

God removed every possible crutch in David's life. He was on the run as the ultimate road warrior without four wheels, trying to stay ahead of the relentless pursuit of King Saul and the army David himself once led.

Desperate times do different things to different people. Some ignore everything that is happening. Some are simply paralyzed. And some do whatever it takes to survive. This is exactly where we find David after he left his best friend, Jonathan.

David showed up to 'the priest' without a fully-baked plan. Ahimelech was terrified by David showing up, and nothing David said or asked for made any sense. Only one thing was consistent: lies!

Out of the mouth of the author of over half the Psalms now came nothing but lies. What happened to the David who wrote "...and in You God I put my trust?"

Stop for a moment. What do you do in moments or seasons of desperate times that seem to call for desperate measures? Do you rip on David or relate to him in his situation?

David was in the presence of the original Ten Commandments of "Thou shall not lie." C'mon, man. Lying? Really? But we often do the very same thing.

David was afraid that if he didn't lie, Ahimelech wouldn't help him. Why did he lie? Because he was afraid, and there goes his faith in God.

After the questionable response of why he was there and alone, David asked about food which is even more strange. "So, what's cookin', man of the cloth?"

He was given consecrated bread, which David ate while he was not clean himself. Again, deception.

What happened to the version of David that wrote "I run to You in times of trouble?"

After chow, David decided to pose one more unusual question (like he hasn't already asked two of them). He asked if the priest had a sword or a spear. Seriously, David? Like the priest is packin' heat? This was when the priest knew something was really off. Here was the most famous and decorated warrior, and he doesn't have a weapon?

David was then transported back in time to the very moments when God brought him into the limelight: the battle against Goliath.

The priest offered the sword of Goliath that David used seven years ago to kill him, and that should've been David's wake-up call. But it wasn't.

David had taken the sword of Goliath as a souvenir after killing him, and who wouldn't? Ultimately, he gave it to the priest to demonstrate it was God's victory, not his own.

What happened to the warrior who, with such confidence from God, spoke to Goliath before taking his life? What happened to the poet who penned words we still read and quote thousands of years later?

He became the man who, during desperate times and through desperate measures, was angry or afraid or alone.

David's lies would have some serious and deadly consequences. Unfortunately, David went from one bad situation right into another one. Ever been there? It's called Duh Town. Population: one more. (All too often, I have a house on the lake there...)

As he fled, David chose a town called Gath. Remember that place? Uh, David, that's the town of Goliath of Gath, the one you killed who also has four giant brothers who are still alive. Yep, *that* Gath. "Hmm. Where did I put those other four stones...?" Minor yet important detail.

David was looking for a place to hide, and he assumed this would be the last place King Saul would go and try to find him. Finally, David was right...but it doesn't mean it was the right place to turn.

Obviously, they recognized him there, and David felt alone and afraid. And what does he choose to do this time? He acted wild. I mean, like certified insane. David had some mad skills (get it, *mad* skills?) Thankfully, they let him go, but our hero showed us a side we were unfamiliar with up to this point in David's life.

And here's the key observation that's easy to overlook when we're angry, afraid, or alone. Notice that never once in these two stories did David do what should've been most natural to him: seek God

> *Every rogue decision we make when we don't seek God will have consequences. Some immediate, most later on. Some affect only you. Other decisions affect people around you.*

Back to the consequences of the first situation. Someone heard just enough from David with Ahimelech to tell Saul, who then executed Ahimelech's entire family along with 85 priests. Wait, stop. David's deception caused how many to die? The innocent priest, his entire family, and all of the other priests. But wait, there's more. Determined King Saul sent his hit men to Nob to slaughter everyone in the village.

One of Ahimelech's sons somehow escaped, found and told David what happened, and David was broken. I can't even imagine the emotions and the weight of responsibility David felt in that very sobering moment. So many people died because he turned inward instead of upward.

Sometimes taking matters into our own hands feels good. It just doesn't often turn out good. Yet we think we know best during desperate times that we feel require our desperate measures.

When we need God the most, we often run from Him the quickest. Sadly, we often run away instead of towards God in these moments.

While it's so easy to see this in the life of those around us, it is nearly impossible to see it in our own life. We feel like things are different in our case. We obviously know what's best. Our only thoughts of God in these moments are "If God were with me, this wouldn't be happening to me." But we know better.

These two stories hit me hard because I have a lifelong pattern of self-reliance, especially when desperate times hit yet again. My choices during these times have caused serious consequences not only to me, but those I love and care about. I often make things worse by going back to one of my road crutches to numb the pain. But it's even in those moments, God gently calls me back to Him.

This was a short, dark, and incredibly painful chapter in David's life, and it happened even after God removed the crutches that he was depending on. God's good like that to remove what He sees is limiting our dependence on Him. But sometimes we just do things the hard way, and God needs to get involved to remind us otherwise.

David eventually wrote when he was older that God is his refuge, a stronghold, which is a place to go to when you're in trouble and need help. But there was a cost for David to learn the dangers of self-reliance.

May the Holy Spirit prompt you right now, as you finish this chapter, to really look at your life and the patterns that lead you away or toward God.

QUESTION

What is your loneliness, anger, or fear causing you to consider on the road that you've never considered before?

Wake-up call question: Who, besides yourself, would your decisions put at risk?

(Answer to the wake-up call question, by the way: the people you love the most and the people that love you the most!)

TODAY'S ROAD PRAYER

God, this was a difficult chapter to read in David's life because I see myself making similar choices when I'm feeling alone, angry, or afraid. I so quickly react to my feelings at the expense of my faith.

But You're there all the more in the desperate times when our emotions are high and our faith is low. Your still small voice is calling out to me to turn to You and trust You in the good *and* the bad.

May I learn to turn to You immediately when I see the clouds get dark and the winds blow so that self-reliance never becomes an option.

I give you the dark days and THIS DAY to become a road warrior after Your own heart.

Write down the potential consequences of taking matters into your own hands on the road.

3.3 DESPERATION

When Life Caves in Around You

READ

So David departed from there and escaped to the cave of Adullam (1 Samuel 22:1 NIV).

I cry out loudly to God, loudly I plead with God for mercy. I spill out all my complaints before him, and spell out my troubles in detail:

As I sink in despair, my spirit ebbing away, you know how I'm feeling, Know the danger I'm in, the traps hidden in my path. Look right, look left— there's not a soul who cares what happens! I'm up against the wall, with no exit— it's just me, all alone. I cry out, God, call out: "You're my last chance, my only hope for life!" Oh listen, please listen; I've never been this low. Rescue me from those who are hunting me down; I'm no match for them. Get me out of this dungeon so I can thank you in public. Your people will form a circle around me and you'll bring me showers of blessing! (Psalm 142 MSG).

REFLECT

The wilderness.
The valley.
The desert.

The cave.

It's the place where time stands still. Dreams come there to die. Hope is a four-letter word. Numbness is the only emotion.

In David's world, it was the loneliest time of his life—and he thought talking to sheep was lonely. It caused him to do some absurd things. The memory of people singing his praises was just that: a faint memory.

His world was now the wilderness, the desert, and a cave.

Maybe this was the original "man cave" but not anything like the term implies now. This was a cave of complete loneliness, where a man questions everyone and everything, and he's always looking over his shoulder.

This was the lowest moment of David's life to date. If you want to know how he really felt, just read the song he composed about it in Psalm 142. He had no security, no food, no one to talk to, no promise to cling to, and no hope that anything would ever change. He was alone in a dark cave, away from everything and everybody he loved.

Everybody except God.

"Geographers have located Adullam about eighteen miles southwest of Jerusalem in the hill country. The hills in this area are riddled with caves. Interestingly, this was not far from the Valley of Elah, the scene of the contest with Goliath. Near the foot of the hill at Adullam there is a fine well of spring water, so the place was ideally suited to David's circumstances. He knew the country well, the hills and valleys providing adequate cover for a guerrilla existence, a good water supply."[48] Ironically, the word Adullam means "sealed off place," much like how David was now feeling.

"That's the way David felt as a cave dweller. In his own words: 'I don't know of a soul on earth who cares for my soul. I am brought very low. Deliver me, Lord.' Yet in the midst of all this, David has not lost sight of God. He cries out for the Lord to deliver him. And here we catch sight of the very heart of the man, that inward place that only God truly sees, that unseen quality that God saw when he chose and anointed the young shepherd boy from Bethlehem."[49]

This part of the story happens to most of us at some point in our lives. It's one we wish never happened, but we wouldn't trade the lessons we learned for anything.

MY STORY

I was hired by a global company headquartered in Madrid, Spain. I was the VP of North America with the task of bringing their product here and building everything from scratch. After ten years in the industry, I was excited for the challenge and the autonomy. It was the most money I had ever made, the highest position, and the most freedom. I was the boss...finally!

I taught headquarters six words that I would repeat seemingly hundreds of times to describe the U.S. market: "twice as long, double the cost."

I was responsible for getting products certified in North America, along with set-up distribution and a reseller channel.

The first six months were surreal. I was hiring my friends as paid consultants, doors were opening, and life was good.

During those early times of getting an established European company ready for the launch here, we were ahead of schedule and under budget with promising days ahead.

Then it happened and without warning. On the last day of quarter three, I got a call from the CEO. The board voted and decided to shut down the North American operations.

Completely stunned, the only word I could utter was "why?"

The response? It was costing too much time and too much money.

Of course.

I asked when it would happen.

The response? Today. Right now. Shut everything down immediately.

The next three months were a nightmare. HQ didn't want me involved in anything, yet my name was on everything. I had to correspond through a lawyer they hired here, and I had to fight for everything: getting paid, severance, shutting things down with revoked authority. Every day the nightmare that was over came back with a few of its friends. The nightmare got stronger, and my strength became weaker.

One moment I was VP, and life was only heading up. The next moment, I was unemployed and in a war. All my time was now fighting the company that had believed in and supported me, seemingly for the long haul.

Few of us have been forced to find refuge in a cave, but all of us have felt some of the same emotions David experienced.

I found myself in my cave. Confused. Hurt. Scared. Alone. Numb.

- I did everything I was asked to do.
- I didn't deserve this treatment.
- I earned this role.

IN THE CAVE

1. Look Outward

You need to come to grips with what has happened around you. This is real and may not change any time soon.

I call this the "assessing the damage" process. Men often go into this mode by default, and it's a good thing. You need to know the collateral damage and take care of any loose ends.

For me, it's making sure my family is safe and taken care of, so they don't have to do anything. At least try and limit their worry. I will pull out a pen and paper to think through everything as much as I can with what I know in the moment.

2. Look Inward

How do I feel about what just happened?

For me, it meant seeing a counselor to process entering this stage of my life (sometimes more than once.) It was actually dealing with the emotions I've been taught to swallow and ignore—the same ones that would have come out in unhealthy ways before.

Take this time to mourn the loss or the change. It's normal. It's important. It's necessary.

3. Look Upward

Sadly, this should be the first direction we turn. (And if we do, it's more like, "God, get me out of this mess!")

But looking upward truly means looking at the situation through God's perspective. How can He use this wilderness, this desert, this cave time to do something in and through you?

Note what David did when he was overwhelmed with unfair treatment and difficult circumstances. First and foremost, David prayed. The Psalms provide an unquestionable testament that David responded to his difficulty with prayer.

David finally came to this direction when he penned the words of Psalm 142. His words are raw. You know he's fully looking outward by the awareness of the danger around him. He's completely looking inward with the awareness of his emotions of feeling confused and abandoned. And he's looking upward by bringing *all* his thoughts and feelings to God, knowing He is David's only hope in times of trouble.

The cave will be one of the hardest times in your life. But it can also be a means that God uses to draw you closer to Him like never before.

THE GIFT OF THE CAVE

It's hard to fathom when you're in the middle of this wilderness season and the cave is dark that good will ever come from this experience. You feel only loss. But it was to the cave that God brought David's family. "When his brothers and his father's household heard about it, they went down to him there" (1 Samuel 22:1). Yep, the ones that overlooked him now come to him. Their motives may be in question since they were literally 'guilty by association' to a known fugitive. But they came, and the cave brought them together.

I've had a similar experience of having my family join me in my cave and our relationship changed in amazing ways.

It was also in the cave that God brought his soon-to-be army. "Everyone in distress, debt, and discontented, gathered to join David in the cave" (1 Samuel 22:2 NIV).

Four hundred men become his personal army. This group would grow to at least six hundred and become an important ingredient of the rest of David's rule over Israel.[50]

Lastly, David poured out his heart to God with incredible honesty and vulnerability, and we read and find hope and comfort in that poetry, thousands of years later. Psalms 27 and 31, and possibly Psalms 57 and 142, were written during this renewal period of faith and confidence in God.

When life caves in around you, the road can be one of the loneliest and most dangerous places to spiral out of control.

Yet it's also the place God can get your attention and teach you to look outward, look inward, and look upward—in ways you've never experienced that can serve you the rest of your life.

QUESTION

Which direction do you need to learn to look: Outward? Inward? Upward?

TODAY'S ROAD PRAYER

God, I'll admit: I have no desire to enter the desert, the wilderness, or the cave on my own. It's lonely, scary, and unknown.

But at some point, I know that life, others, or my own doing may put me in this place where life caves in around me.

If or when this happens, I do know that I will not be alone. You will not only be with me, but You will use this time to develop my heart in ways that can only be done during cave experiences.

May I be open to Your use of the cave times in my life to turn to You and trust You, knowing that You'll use them for Your purposes.

I give you THIS DAY to become a road warrior after Your own heart.

Write down how the direction you chose (outward, inward, upward) can be applied today on the road.

3.4 DISRESPECTED

You Won't Get Away with This Unless...

 **READ**

While David was in the wilderness, he heard that Nabal was shearing sheep. So he sent ten young men and said to them, "Go up to Nabal at Carmel and greet him in my name. Say to him: 'Long life to you! Good health to you and your household! And good health to all that is yours!'"

When David's men arrived, they gave Nabal this message in David's name. Then they waited.

Nabal answered David's servants, "Who is this David? Who is this son of Jesse? Many servants are breaking away from their masters these days. Why should I take my bread and water, and the meat I have slaughtered for my shearers, and give it to men coming from who knows where?"

David's men turned around and went back. When they arrived, they reported every word. David said to his men, "Each of you strap on your sword!" So they did, and David strapped his on as well. About four hundred men went up with David, while two hundred stayed with the supplies.

Abigail rode her donkey down to the other side of the mountain. She met David and his men coming from the other direction.

David was saying, "I protected Nabal's property in the desert. I made sure not one of his sheep was missing. I did all that for nothing. I was good to him, but he was rude to me. I swear, I won't let even one man in Nabal's family live until tomorrow morning."

Just then Abigail arrived. When she saw David, she quickly got off her donkey and bowed down with her face to the ground in front of him. Abigail fell at his feet and said, "Sir, please let me talk to you. Listen to what I say. Blame me for what happened. I didn't see the men you sent. Sir, don't pay any attention to that worthless man, Nabal. His name means 'Foolish,' and that is what he is. The Lord has kept you from killing innocent people. As surely as the Lord lives and you as well, may your enemies and anyone else who wants to harm you be as cursed as Nabal is. Now, I am bringing this gift to you. Please give these things to your men. Please forgive me for doing wrong. I know the Lord will make your family strong because you fight his battles. People will never find anything bad about you as long as you live. If someone chases you to kill you, the Lord your God will save your life. But he will throw away your enemies like a stone from a sling. The Lord promised to do many good things for you, and he will keep his promises. He will make you leader over Israel. So don't do anything that would make you guilty of killing innocent people. Please don't fall into that trap. Please remember me when the Lord blesses you."

David answered Abigail, "Praise the Lord, the God of Israel. Praise God for sending you to meet me" (1 Samuel 25:7–32 NIV).

I can handle a lot, or I like to think I can, but one thing I still don't tolerate well after many decades on this earth is being disrespected, especially in front of other people. #notafan

My pride kicks in, my tongue gets sharp, and the defense attorney in me comes out.

On the road, we have numerous opportunities to get disrespected:

- The annoying seatmate on the plane
- The rude flight attendant
- The server who doesn't get your meal right
- The hotel clerk who doesn't know your status

But what about the big moments that usually happen unexpectedly?

- The client who pushes back
- Your boss who calls you at the worst time on the road
- Your spouse who has "had enough" with *your* kids

David had one of these moments of disrespect…and it was a doozy!

Do you abide by the golden rule until someone hurts you, then you want to change it to "do unto others as they've done to you?"

Or if you can't get back at the person that hurt you, you hurt other people around you. When we feel powerless in one relationship, we often take it out in other relationships.

"The problem with getting even is you're getting even with someone you don't even like."[51]

And this is where we find David in this story. He'd settled into becoming an "assumed protection" and received payment for services rendered. No questions asked.

David and his men lived in the area where Nabal's shepherds grazed their sheep. Seemingly mutual for both David and Nabel. But therein lies the problem.

David came to collect payment from a rich man, Nabal, with this rationale: "Since we've been good to you, be good to us."

Simple. Everyone else appreciates this warrior protecting their wealth.

Not Nabal.

He disrespected David big time in front of his ten men:

- "Who is this David? Who is this son of Jesse?" *I know exactly who you are.*
- "Many servants are breaking away from their masters these days." *You're nothing but a servant to the king and an outlaw, a fugitive, a loner.*

- "Why should I take *my* bread and water, and the meat I have slaughtered for *my* shearers." *What's mine is mine and not a chance I'm sharing anything with you.*
- "And give it to men coming from who knows where?" *I'm not making any charitable donation I didn't authorize, especially to the homeless and desperate.*

Did you catch David's response to the slap in the face in this reading? He said, "each of you strap on your sword." Each of you equals 400 warriors. Mind you, only ten were disrespected.

A little overkill there, David?

Not to David. He was disrespected.

When you're feeling those emotions rise up inside of you, it's easy to feel:

- I'm right. Who do *they* think they are anyway?
- I'm justified. I'm just doing what they've done to me, and they started it!

But we miss a final option in our responses. It is actually a question and the most important one:

"Will this be helpful?"

My counselor, Scott, taught me this question years ago, and I've used it in numerous situations where I've felt attacked or disrespected.

So, I would strap on my sword and rehearse in my mind (and to others) a thousand times, "I'm right and I'm justified!" And I would stop ther.

> *Burn this response into your mind: I may be right, and I may be justified, but will my response be helpful?*

Can you imagine that moment: getting all the boys (400 of them) all riled up and heading with a vengeance to go after one guy.

David *was* right. And he *was* justified. But was his next action going to be helpful in the long run? Would he regret his actions? What was he *really* responding to?

"David's uncontrolled anger related more to an attack on his self-image than on his life."[52]

Then the story takes a surprising twist. Nabal's wife (who was both hot and smart) interceded in a powerful way.

She brought David's crew quite the peace offering (think: major catered event and top-shelf wine) then spoke to David in a way that we all should admire.

Abigail bowed to show respect. Then, she let David know that what he was about to do could be viewed as right. And he was definitely justified.

But then she tactfully asked if it would be helpful for who David is now *and* who he's destined to be years later.

Abigail was already treating him like the man she hoped and thought he'd become.

She spoke to his potential and future, not what he was planning on doing. Whoa, drop the sword, I'm out.

Abigail referenced David fighting Goliath and took him back to the place of his sling and victory. We can only imagine the emotions that created in David. Then, she mentioned knowing he will be king.

Finally, she closed by telling David not to allow "this right and justified action" to become blood on his hands and his conscience.

Stop for a moment and consider the raging emotions David was experiencing on his literal warpath. Remember, women at that time were not generally well-respected themselves, yet this incredible woman of God was used to speak truth into David's life.

God has an Abigail character often there to rescue you in the moment, but it's all in how we respond to them.

How often do we allow the most unlikely person to stop us in our tracks and speak words of truth into our lives? It's not always easy to recognize or accept, but it's both possible and God-honoring.

DAVID DID THREE REMARKABLE THINGS IN HIS MOMENT OF BEING DISRESPECTED:

1. **He paused**: He put the brakes on when God put a barrier (Abigail) in front of him.
2. **He listened**: He humbled himself to receive these words of God through someone else.
3. **He stopped**: He changed his plans and allowed God to change his heart.

The reality is, what you do in this moment of disrespect will be a permanent part of your story. How will you respond?

Will you pause? Will you listen? Will you stop?

You may be right.

You may be justified.

But will your decision be helpful?

Is it any wonder God chose David? What a teachable spirit. He had a sword ready to be unsheathed, and yet he looked at this woman he'd never met before, and he listened to her without interrupting. Then, he changed his entire demeanor and course of action. Talk about a man after God's heart.

(And by the way, David gets the girl in the end. My man.)

RESPOND

QUESTION

1. Do I really want to be even with someone I don't even like?
2. What story do you want to tell? I got even? Predictable and unremarkable.
3. What would it look like to return good for evil? To do nothing is mercy. To do something they don't deserve is grace (choosing to bless them.)

TODAY'S ROAD PRAYER

God, it's so easy to fight back when I'm disrespected. I'm no different than David pulling out the sword and fighting back.

Help me to recognize the rescue efforts you send out that could allow me to pause, listen, and stop.

I want my response to be helpful and not regretful. I want to use even the hard moments of being disrespected to bring me closer to You, knowing You use these difficult moments on the road to grow and strengthen me.

I give you THIS DAY to become a road warrior after Your own heart.

Write down the answers to the three questions above in the RESPOND section. These are big questions and may require some time and some prayer to unpack them, but their answers will be very revealing to you.

3.5 TIMING

Believe It or Not, It's Worth the Wait

He came to the sheep pens along the way; a cave was there, and Saul went in to relieve himself. David and his men were far back in the cave. The men said, "This is the day the Lord spoke of when he said to you, 'I will give your enemy into your hands for you to deal with as you wish.'" Then David crept up unnoticed and cut off a corner of Saul's robe.

Afterward, David was conscience-stricken for having cut off a corner of his robe. He said to his men, "The Lord forbid that I should do such a thing to my master, the Lord's anointed, or lay my hand on him; for he is the anointed of the Lord." With these words, David sharply rebuked his men and did not allow them to attack Saul. And Saul left the cave and went his way (1 Samuel 24:3-7 NIV).

But David said to Abishai, "Don't kill Saul! Anyone who hurts the Lord's chosen king must be punished. As surely as the Lord lives, the Lord himself will punish Saul. Maybe Saul will die naturally or maybe he will be killed in battle. But I pray that the Lord never lets me hurt the Lord's chosen king. Now pick up the spear and waterjug by Saul's head and let's go" (1 Samuel 26: 9-11 ERV).

David was human just like all of us. I don't know what it's like to be on the run for four hours, let alone four long years.

I don't know how I would possibly respond. I get easily worked up on the road when my flight is delayed or my hotel room is not ready. I cannot fathom what my heart would be like after being a loner and fugitive.

Don't forget that David started in solitude as a shepherd, doing the most menial task in the smallest of small towns. He then rose to Patrick Mahomes-level fame with the defeat of Goliath, marrying into the king's family, and winning countless battles resulting in people literally singing his praises.

And now he's been forced out by a horrible boss, ostracized and alone, and questioned by everyone.

You and I would do anything to get out of this season of life—a period of waiting, wondering, and questioning. And if you're anything like me, your mind plays tricks on you. Justifications easily become real possibilities.

David was no different. Not once but twice, David had the perfect opportunity to kill his former boss, King Saul. And I don't mean "looks that could kill."

King Saul stopped everything else in his life and his kingdom to enlist three thousand of his top-tier fighters. Keep in mind, Israel was still at war on its borders. Not only does the king vacate those fights, but he pulled his best soldiers from the front lines for a personal vendetta against David. You wonder how many of those men David led at one time.

I love how real and unfiltered the Bible is. King Saul came into the very cave where David was camping (the original Camp David?) Clueless, Saul walked into the ultimate embarrassing death trap. Can you imagine the amazement of David and his men?

All of a sudden, King Saul disrobed and went to the bathroom, leaving him in a very vulnerable position. Ya think?

Now, David's men could hardly contain themselves, thinking that this could not be easier: King Saul comes to us? And the stories they'd tell of just how they took the king down.

So, what did David do? He "arose and cut off the edge of Saul's robe secretly" (1 Samuel 24:4 NKJV). Can't you see him? (You're smiling.) Saul's there taking care of his business, scrolling his scrolls to see what's trending, and David sneaked up behind him and—snip—ever so silently cut off a piece of his robe!

Instead of gloating or glorying over what he had done, however, David became troubled. It says his "conscience bothered him." He was conscience-stricken.

Why? He could have killed Saul, but he didn't. All he did was cut off part of the king's robe. What's the big deal about a corner of a robe? So, his hem wasn't level anymore. Who's going to notice? See, that's the way we rationalize when we choose to take things into our own hands and our own timing.

"David cut off a part of the king's garment, and now he began to experience justified guilt. You see, when you really want to walk with God, you desire to come to terms with every detail. You get bothered by the little things.

Pause right here. How are you feeling about a soft conscience and heart? Can you relate, or is your conscience reminding you that it's still there and still works?

David said, "That wasn't right. Hey, I can't do that." It bothered him. So he said to his men, "Far be it from me because of the Lord that I should do this thing to my lord, the Lord's anointed, to stretch out my hand against him, since he is the Lord's anointed" (1 Samuel 24:6 KJV). The Lord's anointed? Dude's tried to hang you on a wall with a spear a couple of times and was now out with, I don't know, like 3000 of the best warriors to hunt you down!

But that's what makes David different. And a man after God's own heart.

I can only imagine *that* conversation with his men, after David let

King Saul know he's lucky to be alive. Literally. Obviously, David's men stayed with him and trusted their leader, even when they didn't understand his decisions. They were ready to go home and be the new king's army. Instead, they were back on the run.

Only a short time later, Saul and his army were still pursuing David, even after he took the high road and Saul vowed to "be a better man like David." That promise lasted about as long as a teenager taking a break from looking at their phone these days.

This time, David was camping at the Desert of Ziph, where they could actually see Saul and his 3000 men. David asked Abishai if he wanted to join him in a really bad idea.

Ever been on the receiving side of that kind of question, especially on business travel? Often alcohol is involved. Just sayin'. Abishai said "Sure, I have nothing but time on my hands. What could possibly go wrong?" (Famous last words.) Then David convinced Abishai to sneak into Saul's camp.

Now, here's a little background. The king sleeps in the middle with all his men protecting him, and Saul had his sword in the ground next to his head, just in case. Could there be more protection for King Saul?

So, what was David thinking? What is the plan here, man? Going out for some intel? Mess with Saul's men? Aren't David and his men supposed to be on the run and on the defense?

Or was David finally at a point to take matters into his own hands?

David wanted to get to Saul. The Bible doesn't state his motives, but he's now the one on the offense, intentionally going to Saul. Did he have a change of heart? Why was David flirting with a decision he'd already made once and was now reconsidering?

I'm sure you can relate. We have so many opportunities to flirt with danger on the road. We enter its camp and wonder why things go the way they do.

Abishai wanted to put King Saul's own sword through his heart with David as the last thing Saul saw. Instead, David felt his conscience again and wisely chose to take Saul's spear and water jug...and head to the hills. Literally.

At sunset, David yelled out to Abner and asked him if he's missing anything, alerting Saul and his men about what just happened. Ironically, Saul actually follows through this time and calls off the search.

Saul's parting words, "You will do great things and surely triumph," are more prophetic than Saul could have known or intended. This was to be the last meeting between the two anointed ones. David went on his way with the blessing and protection of Yahweh. Saul returned home, a king in name only.

"The conflict between Saul and David is resolved, the two men are reconciled, and each goes his separate way. But the happy ending is paper-thin, and the sharp edges of history always poke through. David may be bold, handsome, and charismatic, but the Bible allows us to see him as an outlaw, a mercenary, even a mass murderer, and it raises the alarming notion that he was a traitor, too. Even if, as the Bible intends, we fall in love with David—even if we conclude that he acted with such brutality and cunning *only* because he was forced to do so by the aloofness of the Almighty and the homicidal rage of King Saul—the Bible never allows us to forget that he is a Robin Hood with bloodstained hands."[53]

Again, I can't imagine the reaction of David's men. Not only did they want to go home, but they'd bet their life (literally) on David as the next king. And David let this slip—not just once but twice—through his fingers. Worst of all, this "failure" wasn't due to being overpowered or out-strategized; it was because of David's conscience.

Come again? These men would stay on the run, again and again, because of David's conscience.

The human side would make you question why you would continue month after month and year after year with this guy.

But the spiritual side would convince you not only to follow this leader but to learn from him and hope to become like him, a man after God's own heart.

David chose to trust in what Andy Stanley describes as, "'God's will, in God's way, in God's time.' And taking the life of the king would've been 'David's will, in David's way, in David's time.' David refused to replace what God had put in place."[54]

How is your conscience on the road?

When opportunities to go "off-road" appear to you, like King Saul coming to David in the cave, how do you respond?

Or when you pursue the "off-road," going into the middle of the enemy's camp, how do you respond?

Maybe it's been a long time since you've felt your conscience. Maybe everyone around you, like David's men, is telling you it's okay. Or maybe nobody is with you on the road, and no one will ever know. What do you choose?

As a road warrior after God's own heart, you know the answer.

Humanly speaking, David had every right to kill Saul in the cave. Someone was literally trying to kill him, so it would have been self-defense.

But the lesson here is…

God's will.

God's way.

God's time.[55]

> *I will not violate the will of God to gain the blessings or promises of God to get what I deserve, because this is not about me.*

I will choose God's ways, even if I don't understand them.

And I will trust in God's timing, no matter what.

RESPOND

QUESTION

What is God's spirit trying to tell you in your conscience that needs to change?

TODAY'S ROAD PRAYER

God, I want my conscience to be like David's conscience so I hear that still small voice of yours.

To be honest, it's been a while since I've really listened to my conscience. It's usually the first thing I silence, like my phone.

I too easily justify my actions and make it my will and what I want to do, not Your will.

I make it the way I want, not Your way.

I choose my timing, not Your perfect timing.

May You soften my heart today to hear your still small voice and re-awaken my conscience to trust Your Will, Your ways, and Your timing to become a road warrior after Your own heart.

REACT

Write down the one area where God is speaking to your conscience in this moment, and what you need to do about it.

SEASON FOUR
David as a Leader

DAVID AS A LEADER

4.1 CHOICE
Leading What's Given to You Right Now

In the course of time, David inquired of the Lord. "Shall I go up to one of the towns of Judah?" he asked.

The Lord said, "Go up."

David asked, "Where shall I go?"

"To Hebron," the Lord answered.

So David went up there with his two wives, Ahinoam of Jezreel and Abigail, the widow of Nabal of Carmel. David also took the men who were with him, each with his family, and they settled in Hebron and its towns. Then the men of Judah came to Hebron, and there they anointed David king over the tribe of Judah.

Ish-Bosheth son of Saul was forty years old when he became king over Israel, and he reigned two years. The tribe of Judah, however, remained loyal to David. The length of time David was king in Hebron over Judah was seven years and six months (2 Samuel 2:1-4, 10-11 NIV).

The war between the house of Saul and the house of David lasted a long time. David grew stronger and stronger, while the house of Saul grew weaker and weaker (2 Samuel 3:1 NIV).

All the tribes of Israel came to David at Hebron and said, "We are your own flesh and blood. In the past, while Saul was king over us, you were the one who led Israel on their military campaigns. And the Lord said to you, 'You will shepherd my people Israel, and you will become their ruler.'"

When all the elders of Israel had come to King David at Hebron, the king made a covenant with them at Hebron before the Lord, and they anointed David king over Israel.

David was thirty years old when he became king, and he reigned forty years. In Hebron he reigned over Judah seven years and six months, and in Jerusalem he reigned over all Israel and Judah thirty-three years (2 Samuel 5:1-4 MSG).

Have you ever had extreme bad news and extreme good news on the same day? David had one of those days.

The bad news was that his best friend, Jonathan, had been killed in battle. The good news? His arch-enemy and pursuer, King Saul, was also dead.

David mourns the loss of *both*. Huh? It's supposed to be a celebration! David, however, respects the Lord's anointed, something he proved over and over by not taking the life of the king. He's literally shown this respect, even when he would've personally benefitted.

Finally, David's years on the run as a loner and outlaw are finally over. It's a part of his story now and no longer part of his present.

There is a sense of relief that the anointing all those years earlier, when David was still a no-name, is finally a reality. I wonder how many times David wondered if it was really going to come true. We get impatient when God doesn't answer our prayers or dreams, and David had just cause to get a little anxious.

Shepherd to giant killer to warrior to fugitive to king. What a journey! But he hasn't earned the full reward, at least yet. Only one of the twelve tribes recognizes David as king.

I don't know about you, but my attitude of "I want what's mine, and I want the whole thing now" comes out pretty quickly, especially when I've had to wait. And wait. It's ugly, it's hard-wired, and it's selfish. I don't like it and am embarrassed by it when it does come out.

Yet David has a different response. He "inquires of the Lord."

I, too, will often come to the Lord, but it sadly looks a lot different. "God, why is this happening to me? Why didn't I get that position or what I was told would be coming to me? This isn't fair. Fix it. I'm waiting. Still waiting. Fine, I'll just do it myself. Good talk. I'm sure You'll understand. Bless my efforts. Oh, and Amen."

Not David. Our man after God's own heart learned a very valuable lesson as a loner on the run, as a fugitive and outlaw. When we're angry, alone, or afraid, we default to self first. We take matters into our hands and, when it doesn't work out as planned, then "inquire of the Lord."

How easily David could've played "the anointing" card at so many points along the way to being crowned king. For the road warrior, anointing looks like "entitled due to status."

He could've had an attitude with his horrible boss, knowing he was going to take his place one day. But he didn't. What he *did* do was serve as a servant at every opportunity, big or small, that was given to him.

He could've taken the life of King Saul twice, but he didn't. What he *did* do was respond to his conscience and that "still small voice" of God's spirit, instead of David's will, David's way, in David's time.

He could've marched into town for his crown-fitting the moment he found out King Saul was killed. But he didn't. What he *did* do was mourn the loss of God's anointed and his best friend, then he prayed to God for what he should do next.

Ironically, David who was anointed 'the next king' is only given part of the overall kingdom, and the smallest part. Some guy named Ish-Bosheth gets the real gig, since he was a son of Saul. And he didn't even have a cool name! (Don't you just love when someone gets the job because of a convenient connection?)

"Though the way for David to proceed is clear in theory, it is also filled with danger. The Philistines have demonstrated their superiority in the north in addition to their traditional strongholds in the southwest. Sauls's son, Ish-Bosheth, has legitimate claims from a human perspective (over the northern tribes especially.) If David is to become king of a unified Israel, he will need more wisdom than he can conjure on his own."[56]

There was war between David's side (Judah) and Ishbosheth's (Israel) for years, and it was ugly. Here David was still fighting for what is rightfully his and had to wait. Again.

Let me stop for a moment and ask you, how would you respond if you waited *this long* for a promotion—"the" promotion—and you're only given part of it?

And the real kicker here is that David had this small gig for over seven years! Not seven weeks or seven months, but over seven years.

I don't want this point to get lost in the mix. David finally gets the position that is rightfully his, but it's incomplete. A *sort-of* promotion. Yet, he leads like he has the entire position at hand.

This response takes a man after God's own heart to pull off.

"God's will.

God's way.

God's timing."[57]

Finally, after seven years, the entire kingdom is united, and David officially becomes the big boss. The long journey of anointing to full kingship is finally here.

THREE LEADERSHIP LESSONS TO BE LEARNED AND APPLIED:

- *Lead When You Can*: You don't know when an opportunity to lead in any capacity is available, so lead when it's given to you. It may not be ideal, maybe far from it. But David led in every opportunity given to him.
- *Lead Where You Are*: This may not be the optimal location, but that doesn't matter in leadership. What matters is where

you are in that moment. David stepped up in each location where leadership was required.

- **Lead *What You Have***: It may not be what you were promised or what you hoped for, but lead whomever you've been given and make the most of it. David even led a group of less-than-ideal soldiers in the wilderness, but he was there and he led.

I've had numerous opportunities to lead people and teams through the years. Most often, my opportunities and my expectations were miles apart. I wanted more and was given less. I was promised something on the front end that never panned out on the back end. I didn't always lead the best due to my expectations. Or it was easy to take a bad attitude and sulk. As a result, my leadership and my results suffered.

My father always taught me to be "faithful in the little things" for two reasons:

1. You don't know who's watching.
2. You should honor God in everything you do.

David was a perfect example of being faithful in the little things. As a result, God firmly planted him into the first major leadership role of his anointing.

May you lead when you can, where you are, and with what you have right now.

QUESTION

If you're leading people, how are your attitude and your expectations right now?

TODAY'S ROAD PRAYER

God, the opportunity to lead is a gift from You.

But I don't always see it that way, and I often let my expectations affect me instead of leaning into the opportunity.

I give you THIS DAY to become a road warrior after Your own heart.

Write down how you need to start, or continue, to be faithful in the little things in your leadership right now.

4.2 NEVERTHELESS

Defeating the Strongholds in Your Life

 **READ**

The king and his men marched to Jerusalem to attack the Jebusites, who lived there. The Jebusites said to David, "You will not get in here; even the blind and the lame can ward you off." They thought, "David cannot get in here." Nevertheless, David captured the fortress of Zion—the City of David.

On that day David had said, "Anyone who conquers the Jebusites will have to use the water shaft to reach those lame and blind who are David's enemies." That is why they say, "The blind and lame will not enter the palace."

David then took up residence in the fortress and called it the City of David. He built up the area around it, from the terraces inward. And he became more and more powerful, because the Lord God Almighty was with him (2 Samuel 5: 6-9 NIV).

 **REFLECT**

What is one weakness, bad habit, or rotten attitude that you're struggling with that *owns* you right now? Where does the evil one have a stronghold within you? Ahh, there is a fitting word.

Stronghold: a fortress, a citadel with thick walls and tall gates.

David was finally king over all of Israel. Now, he needed a strategic capital city. He knew exactly where he wanted it, and in classic David style, he wanted to capture it in a hostile takeover.

As with all great leaders, the first decisions are the most important. They signal all that is to come. David's first royal decisions were wise beyond his years.

"David knew where it had to be. All he had to do was capture a city that had never been taken; no less than David himself was the choice of God, so Jebus was the choice of God, and David knew it."[58]

This fortress was inhabited by the Jebusites. "No one bothers them. Philistines fight the Amalekites. Amalekites fight the Hebrews. But the Jebusites? They are a coiled rattlesnake in the desert. Everyone leaves them alone.

Everyone, that is, except David. The just-crowned king of Israel has his eye on Jerusalem, the Fortress at Zion. He's inherited a divided kingdom. The people need not just a strong leader, but strong headquarters. David's present base of Hebron sits too far south to enlist the loyalties of the northern tribes. But if he moves north, he'll isolate the south. He seeks a neutral, centralized city."[59]

"Unlike the other cities of Canaan, Jerusalem had beaten back the Israelite armies under the command of Joshua during the invasion and conquest that first established Israelite sovereignty: 'And as for the Jebusites, the inhabitants of Jerusalem, the children of Judah could not drive them out' (Joshua 15:63 KJV). To make Jerusalem the capital of his new monarchy, David would have to succeed where the mighty Joshua had failed."[60]

"Jerusalem is ideal for its natural defenses, central location, and lack of previous attachment to the tribes of Israel. Without doubt, Jerusalem is the most important city in the Bible. It is mentioned over eight hundred times in the Bible. The name *Jerusalem* itself is known from Egyptian texts as old as nineteenth century B.C., hundreds of years before David's time."[61]

"He wants Jerusalem. We can only wonder how many times he's stared at these impenetrable walls. He grew up in Bethlehem, only a day's walk to the south. He hid in the caves in the region of En Gedi, not far south. Surely, he noticed Jerusalem. Somewhere he pegged the place as the perfect capital. The crown had scarcely been resized for him when he set his eyes on his newest Goliath."[62]

This surprisingly short story references one specific word mentioned twice: *stronghold*. In verse 7, "David took the stronghold," and in verse 9, "David dwelt in the stronghold."

Jebusite soldiers had more than enough time to direct arrows at any would-be wall climbers from their rooftop view. And discouraging? Just listen to the way the city-dwellers taunted David.

"You'll never get in here...Even the blind and lame could keep you out!" (2 Samuel 5:6 NLT).

The Jebusites pour trash talk on David like Satan dumps buckets of discouragement on you:

- You're a no-name and will always be a no-name.
- You're a loner on the road and nobody really wants to be with you unless you're buying dinner or drinks.
- You'll never overcome your bad habits that nobody else at home knows about

David wanted victory in a major area of his life but came across a challenge, one that not only seemed insurmountable but mocked back at him.

If you've heard the kind of mocking David heard, your story needs the word that exists in David's story. Did you see it? Most hurry past it. Be aware of your Spidey-senses and catch this long and incredibly potent twelve letter word: NEVERTHELESS.

"Nevertheless David took the stronghold . . ."

"Wouldn't you love God to write a *nevertheless* in your biography? Born to alcoholics, *nevertheless* she lead a sober life. Never went to college, *nevertheless* he mastered a trade. Didn't read the Bible until retirement age, *nevertheless* he came to a deep and abiding faith. [Struggled with a secret sin on the road for years, *nevertheless* God gave him victory.]

David turns a deaf ear to old voices. Those mockers strutting on the wall tops? David ignores them. He dismisses their words and goes about his work."[63]

I'm a fighter and not a fan of disrespect and insults. Too often I would've responded back with some sarcastic well-thought-through response that shuts the other side down and makes their only response "Well, my dad can beat up your dad." Not David. He was looking for the nevertheless in this stronghold.

"Nehemiah, on these same walls, took an identical approach. In his case, however, he was atop the stones, and the mockers stood at the base. Fast-forward 500 years from David's time, and you will see that the bulwarks of Jerusalem are in ruins, and many of her people are in captivity. Nehemiah heads up a building program to restore the fortifications. Critics tell him to stop. They plan to interfere with his work. They list all the reasons the stones can't and shouldn't be re-stacked. But Nehemiah won't listen to them. 'I am doing a great work, so that I cannot come down. Why should the work cease while I leave it and go down to you?' (Nehemiah 6:3 KJV)"[64]

Love me some Nehemiah putting his priorities in perspective.

David could've easily tried the hard way, you know, the way everyone else tries and fails. But he had to find another way. The problem all too often is the first battle, the one in your head.

"Two types of thoughts continually vie for your attention.

One says, 'Yes you can.' The other says, 'No you can't.'

One says, 'God will help you.' The other lies, 'God has left you.'

One speaks the language of heaven; the other deceives in the vernacular of the Jebusites. One proclaims God's strengths; the other lists your failures.

One longs to build you up; the other seeks to tear you down.

And here's the great news: you select the voice you hear. Why listen to the mockers? Why heed their voices? Why give ear to pea-brains and scoffers when you can, with the same ear, listen to the voice of God?"[65]

David didn't need to listen to other voices here. He knew his men would never breach the walls through brute force. The way into the city was through the water tunnel. After sending Joab and his soldiers up from the inside, the way was open for David's army. It was a bloody battle, but short-lived. David now had a new capital for the new nation. He even gave it a new name: Jerusalem.

"Do what David did. Turn a deaf ear to old voices. And, as you do, open your eyes to new choices. When everyone else saw walls, David saw tunnels. Others focused on the obvious. David searched for the unusual. Since he did what no one expected, he achieved what no one imagined."[66]

So, how does this apply to the life of the spiritual road warrior?

If the wall is too high, try a tunnel.

There are battles on the road few understand, let alone ever experience. But we do. And they're real, relentless, and often paralyzing. They're waiting for us on every trip no matter where we are. Different city, same stronghold.

For Paul, a business traveler, his stronghold was porn. He did great until he was alone in his hotel room. Lonely, curious, and tempted. No matter the city, that quiet hotel room became his biggest challenge. He tried everything and would even have a victory night from time-to-time. But this stronghold would return every single road trip.

He was climbing a wall when he needed to look for a tunnel. He needed his *nevertheless* in his own story. Paul was fighting this battle alone until he opened up to the help of others. He saw a Christian counselor. He told the guys in his small group. He put a filter on his computer, phone, and tablet. He prepared for the challenging moment and chose to read his Bible and quote scripture in these difficult moments. He shed light in this dark area. And everything changed. Was it easy? Nope. Was it quick? Nowhere close. But was there victory? Absolutely.

Who knows, you may be a prayer away from a *nevertheless*. God loves to give them if you're only willing to receive them.

The end reality is the capture of Jerusalem was entirely a private affair of David's. "And David dwelt in the stronghold and called it the City of David" (2 Samuel 5:9 NKJV).

May you find your *nevertheless* in the stronghold in your road life.

May you find this victory in your life moving forward as you seek to become a road warrior after God's own heart.

QUESTION

What stronghold came to mind as you read this chapter today?

TODAY'S ROAD PRAYER

God, most don't know the battles of business travel. But You do.

You know my own personal struggles with _____
. I'm bringing them into the light right now and seeking Your intervention in my stronghold.

I want to be able to say "Nevertheless I took the stronghold . . ." But I need Your strength to find a different approach. I need a tunnel, not a wall, to find victory in this area.

I give you THIS DAY and THIS STRONGHOLD and turn it into a NEVERTHELESS to become a road warrior after Your own heart.

Pray and then write down how you can find a tunnel instead of climbing the wall of your stronghold so that you can find your nevertheless victory that begins today.

4.3 COMPASSION

A Surprising and Impressive Act of Kindness

One day David asked, "Is there anyone left of Saul's family? If so, I'd like to show him some kindness in honor of Jonathan."

It happened that a servant from Saul's household named Ziba was there. They called him into David's presence. The king asked him, "Are you Ziba?"

"Yes sir," he replied.

The king asked, "Is there anyone left from the family of Saul to whom I can show some godly kindness?"

Ziba told the king, "Yes, there is Jonathan's son, lame in both feet."

"Where is he?"

"He's living at the home of Makir son of Ammiel in Lo Debar."

King David didn't lose a minute. He sent and got him from the home of Makir son of Ammiel in Lo Debar.

When Mephibosheth son of Jonathan (who was the son of Saul), came before David, he bowed deeply, abasing himself, honoring David.

David spoke his name: "Mephibosheth."

"Yes sir?"

"Don't be frightened," said David. "I'd like to do something special for you in memory of your father Jonathan. To begin with, I'm returning to you all the properties of your grandfather Saul. Furthermore, from now on you'll take all your meals at my table."

Shuffling and stammering, not looking him in the eye, Mephibosheth said, "Who am I that you pay attention to a stray dog like me?"

David then called in Ziba, Saul's right-hand man, and told him, "Everything that belonged to Saul and his family, I've handed over to your master's grandson. You and your sons and your servants will work his land and bring in the produce, provisions for your master's grandson. Mephibosheth himself, your master's grandson, from now on will take all his meals at my table." Ziba had fifteen sons and twenty servants.

"All that my master the king has ordered his servant," answered Ziba, "your servant will surely do."

And Mephibosheth ate at David's table, just like one of the royal family. Mephibosheth also had a small son named Mica. All who were part of Ziba's household were now the servants of Mephibosheth (2 Samuel 4:1-12 MSG).

REFLECT

"Some people when they become successful use all their energy and resources protecting and guarding their success. Others go out of their way looking for ways to share what they have, extending the realm of blessing. David went looking for ways to be generous."[67]

Sadly, I have my own share of stories of successful people protecting and guarding their success. But this one hidden and often overlooked story in the life of David as a leader is so relevant to a road warrior after God's own heart. No one expected him to be committed to an old promise and show this level of compassion.

So, what's the backstory with David and this guy whose name we can't pronounce?

"Finally, the days of ducking Saul are a distant memory. But something stirs one of them. A comment, perhaps, resurrects an old conversation. Maybe a familiar face jars a dated decision. In the midst of his new life, David remembers a promise from his old one: 'Is there still anyone who is left of the house of Saul, that I may show him kindness for Jonathan's sake?' (2 Samuel. 9:1 NIV)

When Saul threatened to kill David, Jonathan sought to save him. Jonathan succeeded and then made this request: 'If I make it through this alive, continue to be my covenant friend. And if I die, keep the covenant friendship with my family—forever' (1 Samuel 20:14–15 MSG). Jonathan does die. But David's covenant does not. No one would have thought twice had he let it. David has many reasons to forget the vow he made with Jonathan. The two were young and idealistic.

Who keeps the promises of youth? Saul was cruel and relentless. Who honors the children of a nemesis?"[68]

Just think about this for a moment. David met his covenant already with Jonathan, nobody knows nor cares about this possible heir, yet David went searching as the new king to still show compassion on someone else.

Who does that?

A man after God's own heart. It's those types of thoughts and actions that reveal this side of David that so pleased God.

David asked around the palace if anyone could help him on this seemingly random goose chase. Finding a descendant of Jonathan wasn't easy. Could you imagine being asked this question by the king?

Since the custom was to kill anyone from a previous dynasty, such individuals were either exterminated or they hid for the rest of their lives. And that's what this man had done. He had hidden himself away, and the only one who knew his actual location was an old servant of Saul named Ziba. He knew of a son of Jonathan named Mephibosheth that was still alive. (What great names! Needing ideas on what to name your newborns? Try Ziba and Mephibosheth. They'll stand out in their class.)

Ziba asked if David was sure he wanted the likes of this "kind of person," especially in the palace around the chosen few. Great, David had an out if he wanted it. But do you really think he takes it?

A LITTLE BACKSTORY ON MEPHIBOSHETH

When Mephibosheth was five years old, his father and grandfather died at the hands of the Philistines. One of the nurses picked up the boy who was in her care and ran for both of their lives. As she hurried, she probably tripped, and the boy tumbled out of her arms. I can't even imagine that moment for her. As a result of that fall, he was permanently disabled and had been hiding away ever since fearing for his life.

In an act of mercy, some servants carried him across the Jordan River to a literal desert town called Lo Debar. He hid there first in fear of the Philistines, then for fear of David. To say this kid grew up with some major fear issues is an understatement. The last thing he wanted to see at his door was someone from the king. But that was exactly what happened.

Mephibosheth's resume:

- Born rightful heir to the throne
- Victimized by a fall not of his doing
- Left alone in a foreign land
- Living under a constant threat of death

David doesn't hesitate. He sends his black Uber stretch chariot to pick up Jonathan's son.

Can you imagine what Mephibosheth was thinking and feeling on his way to the palace? This was Dead Man Walking...and he couldn't even walk. Could it get any worse?

Faster than you can say Mephibosheth twice, he was promoted from Lo Debar to High Delife and the king's table. Adios, obscurity. Hello, royalty!

It's worth mentioning that David could have taken the easy way out and just sent money to Lo Debar. A pension or scholarship for life would have more than met his obligation to his friend. But David gave Jonathan's son more than a slush fund; he gave him a place at the king's table. A place to be noticed, loved, and finally matter to someone. And quite a someone it was: the king. For the first time ever, Mephibosheth wasn't ashamed and scared but proud and loved.

David's first word to Mephibosheth was the speaking of his name (2 Samuel 4:6). Mephibosheth was recognized as a person. He was not a nameless exile; he was not a subcategory of victim. He had a name, and David went to the trouble to learn it: Mephibosheth. If there was any shame or dishonor associated with this name through the years, it could not be more the opposite moving forward. The name is used seven times in this story of their meeting, without a hint of denigration in the usage. If I were David, the new kid in the house would be getting a nickname. "Hey, Phibs" or "Sheth, my man." And could you imagine how personal his name would've felt to him for the first time in his life?

"Don't miss this point: Mephibosheth has every reason to be deathly afraid of David at that moment. He has no reason to think that David is not out to get rid of him, the last vestige of Saul's family and therefore a potential rival to David's claim to the throne. And then he is disarmed and prepared for inclusion into the friendship-covenant that his father Jonathan and David had made before his birth. David puts content into the word loyal-love when he turns over to Mephibosheth all the lands of his grandfather Saul so that he will have an independent income, assigns Ziba, once servant to Saul, to manage the farms and take care of his affairs, and then brings Mephibosheth into his household as one of the family."[69]

I could only imagine the stories David could've told about Mephibosheth's dad. Stories he had never heard that would bring him closer to a father who was no longer around. I cherish these moments: stories shared by someone who knew my father. They let me in on moments I would never know unless they took the time to tell me. If they only knew how much those memories meant to me. How they brought a smile to my face, made me laugh, and made me proud.

And this is exactly the gift David gave to his best friend's son. "David is a man of loyalty. He is not 'kind' to everyone, but he is loyal to those to whom he has obligation. To outsiders he can be brutal and ruthless (2 Samuel 8:2,5), but to those in the scope of his promise he is gracious and steadfast."[70]

"Look closely at the family portrait hanging over David's fireplace; you'll see the grinning graduate of Lo Debar High School. David sits enthroned in the center, with of course, far too many wives. Just in front of tanned and handsome Absalom, right next to the drop-dead beauty of Tamar, down the row from bookish Solomon, you'll see Mephibosheth, the grandson of Saul, the son of Jonathan, leaning on his crutches and smiling as if he's just won the Jerusalem lottery. Which indeed he had. The kid who had no legs to stand on has everything to live for. Why? Because he impressed David? Convinced David? Coerced David? No, Mephibosheth did nothing. A promise prompted David. The king is kind, not because the boy is deserving, but because the promise is enduring."[71]

"Mephibosheth had nothing, deserved nothing, could repay nothing…in fact, didn't even try to win the king's favor…David restored Mephibosheth from a place of barrenness to a place of honor…Mephibosheth's disability was a constant reminder of grace… When Mephibosheth sat down at the table of the king, he was treated just like any other son of the king."[72]

How powerful of a picture! God did the very same thing to us. Do you truly grasp that gift? And how often do we not feel the weight of this rescue and allow ourselves to be humbled by the life change that the God of the Universe gave us. He cares that much for us that He wants us to have a seat at His table.

This ending to the story still blows me away. It's a side of David that most of us never knew but truly shows the man after God's own heart. May we all look for opportunities to serve and bless people on the road with this same grace God has given to us.

QUESTION

Who could you show compassion to on the road today that doesn't deserve it, but could surely use it?

TODAY'S ROAD PRAYER

God, what a story of how David cared that much about others to demonstrate a love that could only come from You.

May I see myself in Mephibosheth first and foremost, that You love me that much to bring me out of obscurity and fear to a seat at Your table.

But may I also see those all around me today: those at the airport, on the plane, who serve my meals and clean my room. May You open my eyes to show compassion when it's not expected but greatly appreciated. And may I notice your prompting and act quickly.

I give you THIS DAY to become a road warrior after Your own heart.

Write down who could come across your path today that you could show a lasting act of compassion. Then prepare yourself for how you could act immediately when the moment arises.

4.4 COUNSELOR

The Invaluable Role of a Trusted Advisor

 **READ**

"You're the man!" said Nathan. "And here's what God, the God of Israel, has to say to you: I made you king over Israel. I freed you from the fist of Saul. I gave you your master's daughter and other wives to have and to hold. I gave you both Israel and Judah. And if that hadn't been enough, I'd have gladly thrown in much more. So why have you treated the word of God with brazen contempt, doing this great evil? You murdered Uriah the Hittite, then took his wife as your wife. Worse, you killed him with an Ammonite sword! And now, because you treated God with such contempt and took Uriah the Hittite's wife as your wife, killing and murder will continually plague your family. This is God speaking, remember! I'll make trouble for you out of your own family. I'll take your wives from right out in front of you. I'll give them to some neighbor, and he'll go to bed with them openly. You did your deed in secret; I'm doing mine with the whole country watching!"

Then David confessed to Nathan, "I've sinned against God."

Nathan pronounced, "Yes, but that's not the last word. God forgives your sin. You won't die for it. But because of your blasphemous behavior, the son born to you will die" (2 Samuel 12:7-14 MSG).

After the king was settled in his palace and the Lord had given him rest from all his enemies around him, he said to Nathan the prophet, "Here I am, living in a house of cedar, while the ark of God remains in a tent."

Nathan replied, "Whatever you have in mind, go ahead and do it, for the Lord is with you."

But that night the word of the Lord came to Nathan, saying:

"Go and tell my servant David, 'This is what the Lord says: Are you the one to build me a house to dwell in? I have not dwelt in a house from the day I brought the Israelites up out of Egypt to this day. I have been moving from place to place with a tent as my dwelling. Wherever I have moved with all the Israelites, did I ever say to any of their rulers whom I commanded to shepherd my people Israel, Why have you not built me a house of cedar?'" (2 Samuel 7:1-7 NASB).

If you're like most of mankind, you're not a big fan of confrontations. I've had them happen a few times, and a couple of them were biggies. Life altering, from this moment forward. Yet, God used key people to stop my actions from becoming destructive.

Few Bible characters have a Nathan in their lives. Most of us know of Nathan thanks to the second most popular story in the life of David (after killing Goliath): adultery with Bathsheba.

Maybe you assumed like I did that this was the only time Nathan appears in a major role in the life of David. In fact, Nathan appeared before David in a different situation dealing not with sin, but with ambition and pride. Let's start with this one since we may relate to it right away.

David was king over all of Israel. He'd defeated every giant. He'd conquered every enemy. To put it bluntly, David was looking for a new conquest. He wanted something to do that has meaning. So, he called Nathan the Prophet, his trusted advisor and counselor, a White House chaplain of sorts, and let him in on what's he was thinking.

David, to his credit, looked at all that God has blessed him with told Nathan that it really bothered him that the ark of the covenant was still being housed in some oversized tent. This didn't sit well with David, who shared with Nathan his plans to build a temple for the ark. Whaddya think, Nate?

Surprisingly, Nathan responded, "Yes, that's a great idea! You should definitely build one." Then he added, "God is with you on this."

Except He wasn't exactly. God never told Nathan that, and had to remind the prophet that he had it all backwards. First God speaks, then the prophet…not the other way around. In fact, God had a very different message for David.

God, through Nathan, told David "Love your vision, but not yet and not you" (Buckley paraphrase). He also reminded David of where He had taken him to where he was right now, and God told him that He will raise up one of David's sons to see this vision through to completion.

"God reserved this great accomplishment for David's son—not out of punishment or spite, but out of love. God is extremely aware of the pride men can feel when they survey all they have supposedly accomplished."[73]

But this is still humbling and a pride check. I for one do *not* like to be told "no" for any reason, especially if I think it's a good idea.

For David's sake, God allowed him to make the plans. This is ironic and therapeutic because David's part would be behind-the-scenes only with no glory—something new for David. His pride was saved here. But his next major recorded encounter with Nathan would end differently.

Remember, David had a counselor that showed up twice in his life for two very different and specific purposes:

1. Correction (Re-direction)
2. Confrontation (Sin)

I'm not sure how confrontation has played in your own life, or if it's ever led to a situation that had major consequences.

This happened to me and, sadly, my impulse was to protect

myself. I was no longer the no-name but the warrior and leader where confrontation always looks and feels differently. My goal was not confession, but protection. I needed to find out what they knew and quickly. I needed to know what I was actually caught for, and what I needed to admit (preferably as little as possible.) #HorriblePlan

I hate this natural defense in me. I see it in some of my kids and am trying to break the sins of the father. And oh, how I despise it in others, especially when I know far more than they know. Yet, I still so easily succumb to self-protection before confession. God help me.

"At this midpoint of David's life, his complexity is confusing. What exactly was David? He was a shepherd. A politician. A leader. A rebel guerrilla leader. A hired mercenary working for the enemy. A unifier. A psalm writer. A husband. An adulterer. A murderer."[74] It's unthinkable that this larger-than-life Biblical hero would have a loyal friend killed in a pathetic attempt at a cover-up. The brazen affair was bad enough. To commit murder just to save yourself the shame is a whole different breed of sin."

Maybe nobody else noticed, or so David thinks. But God did, and He designed a strategy, the ultimate bait-and-switch and slight of hand, to bring David to his knees. God is awfully good at that.

Consider this: if you think David's life was enjoyable and that he had long stress-free nights with his new wife, free of guilt, and not a care in this world during those months that followed, then simply review Psalm 32.

"For the better part of a year, David lived a life of hypocrisy and deception. His world became a world of guarded, miserable secrecy. Looking at the situation during that period, as the days and months passed, one might have thought that the holy God of heaven was asleep, or at least was letting it pass—that sin does actually pay, that there are no wages."[75]

God knows this about David, especially considering how long he had had the opportunity to confess and take responsibility for his actions. But he didn't—week after week, month after month. David somehow thinks he's gotten away with his sin of adultery, deception, using people, and even murder. His mind and body knew otherwise, with the stress that was a result.

Does this resemble you? In one sense, I point at David and think, "How do you think you could possibly get away with this, especially with so many other people involved?" Yet on the other hand, I hurt for the guy…because I was *that* guy. I've made mistakes that I've tried to cover up. Ugh, the lies we can find ourselves in to cover our own sinful actions.

But God loves us too much to keep us in this dark place. One of the hardest verses in the Bible says this: "No discipline seems pleasant at the time but painful. Later, of course, it pays off big-time, for it's the well-trained who find themselves mature in their relationship with God" (Hebrews 12:11 MSG). And discipline was exactly what was ahead for David.

God chose to use Nathan in a very unique and unassuming way to get David's attention and avoid denial and partial confession. God gave Nathan the wisdom and ability to become a master storyteller. He creatively involved and captivated David to the point of extreme emotion to offer this surprise ending, something that any streaming service would go over-and-above to try to do.

You see, when you need to confront someone who has the power and ability to seemingly get away with sin as extreme as David's, you need a different approach. Attack from a different angle. A slingshot, not a sword. A sneak attack, not full-on hand-to-hand combat. And you may know this similar ability as David with your role as a leader, a road warrior.

Masterfully as Nathan drew David in, David was clueless that this story was actually his story. His judgement on the "hypothetical" situation was what should be done in his *real* situation.

Let's pause for a second. Can you imagine if you're Nathan and having to confront "the king" with that revelation bomb? Would this be your last day on earth if David doesn't like what he hears?

"Hey Nate, thanks for the story but not liking what I'm hearing."

"Hey Joe (short for Joab), take Nate out, and I don't mean for dinner."

Nathan had a lot to lose.

We don't know if he's seen Nathan at any point since the carnage he left from his deception, lust, and manipulation. But we do know that David walked right into this short mini-series of a story that captivates and ultimately captures him, in more ways than one.

Nathan must have thought through how he would present this matter to David because his opening words were both thoughtful and brilliant. Because of the story-approach, David was drawn in and at the same time disarmed of all defenses. Every part of this story, David was just beside himself with anger and judgement. In mere moments, he would be blind-sided. The sin he thought was ancient history would change the rest of his history, and not for the better.

Nathan then paused like a defense attorney on his closing argument with four short, powerful words:

You. Are. That. Man.

Boom. I've had those four words said to me. In that moment, when you know there is no escape, there can only be admission, with a slight alteration of the words:

I. Am. That. Man.

David didn't fight the confrontation. He's beyond denial or partial confession. Nathan knew too much, and he knew everything in great detail. Nathan had the ultimate "insider information."

Ever been there?

Maybe it's a spouse. Maybe it's a boss. Possibly a friend.

This was not a momentary mistake. He didn't stumble into the sin. He willfully and knowingly walked into the sin with Bathsheba, killed her husband (at least indirectly), and deliberately lived a lie during the months that followed.

"It is worth noticing that Nathan didn't come on his own; he was sent by God: 'Then the LORD sent Nathan to David.' I think the most important word in that sentence is the first one, 'then.' God's timing is absolutely incredible. When was he sent? Right after the act of adultery? No. Right after Bathsheba said, 'I am pregnant'?

Nope. Right after he murdered Uriah? Nada. Right after he married Uriah's pregnant widow? Still a no. Right after the birth of the baby? No. It's believed by some Old Testament scholars that there was at least a twelve-month interval that passed before Nathan paid the visit. God waited until just the right time. He let the grinding wheels of sin do their full work and then He stepped in."[76]

Also, notice *who* God chose for the delivery of this message. David knew Nathan well. Nathan had earned David's trust and respect over their years of interacting with each other. Right time, right person.

"At that point, Nathan's mission is complete. End of confrontation. Nathan stands, turns around, walks to the door, opens it, steps through, closes it—and David is left alone. Perhaps it was that same evening that he wrote Psalm 51. What relief forgiveness provided!"[77]

None of us wants a Nathan in our lives for correction or confrontation. But oh, how we need one, spiritual road warriors. This chapter is about the critical role of having a Nathan in our lives and in our junk. But don't miss that we should also learn from David and how he handled confrontation.

May you be challenged and inspired by both of these vitally important lessons from David's life.

QUESTION

How do you respond when confronted? Does it need to change so you can become a road warrior after God's own heart?

TODAY'S ROAD PRAYER

God, it's easy to fall into sin on the road and not let anyone know about it. It's even easier to justify my actions and believe the lie of the evil one: that it's no big deal and I need and desire whatever sin I fall into on the road.

But You know, and it matters to You. In fact, it breaks Your heart and creates separation between You and me.

I need a Nathan in my life. May I be open to that person and their correction and confrontation.

May I soften my heart to Your still small voice long before I need intervention and severe consequences. I ask You to help me learn from this story and what I now need in my life.

I give you THIS DAY to become a road warrior after Your own heart.

Who is the Nathan in your life right now? If you don't have one, who could play that role?

4.5 HUMBLED

Selfish Decisions with Deadly Consequences

So David gave orders to Joab and the army officers under him, "Canvass all the tribes of Israel, from Dan to Beersheba, and get a count of the population. I want to know the number."

But Joab resisted the king: "May your God multiply people by the hundreds right before the eyes of my master the king, but why on earth would you do a thing like this?"

Nevertheless, the king insisted, so Joab and the army officers left the to take a census of Israel.

But when it was all done, David was overwhelmed with guilt because he had counted the people, replacing trust with statistics. And David prayed to God, "I have sinned badly in what I have just done. But now God forgive my guilt—I've been really careless.."

When David got up the next morning, the word of God had already come to Gad the prophet, David's spiritual advisor, "Go and give David this message: 'God has spoken thus: There are three things I can do to you; choose one out of the three and I'll see that it's done.'"

Gad came to deliver the message: "Do you want three years of famine in the land, or three months of running from your enemies while they chase you down, or three days of an epidemic on the country? Think it over and make up your mind. What shall I tell the one who sent me?"

David told Gad, "They're all terrible! But I'd rather be punished by God, whose mercy is great, than fall into human hands" (2 Samuel 24:2-4, 10-14 MSG).

How many times in business have you questioned a decision by your company or your boss? On the outside, the decision is clearly inconsistent or a waste of time, even selfish. But to those making the decision, they see nothing but clarity and forward motion.

I've found myself on both sides of this corporate fence. Both times, I was certain I was right. The difficult part is when you're in leadership and your decision is ignored by those around you—an action that would directly affect the very people you're leading.

At first glance, this event seems like an odd story in general, and it's one that's easily overlooked in the big picture of the six seasons of David's life. However, when the man after God's own heart deliberately ignores the counsel around him, the story proves critical because his decision will ultimately affect everyone.

King David decides to take a census at the very end of his rule as a leader. Note the timing. C'mon, David. By now, you should know better.

"A census is a survey that counts the number of people in a given category, who live in a certain territory, who belong to a certain demographic group, or who live under a specified authority. History's most famous census was the one that coincided with the birth of Jesus. But the process was already quite old by that time. Archeologists have found census records produced thousands of years before Christ."[78] Interesting detail.

An entire book of the Bible is devoted to the results of Israel's census after the Exodus. It is the aptly named Book of Numbers (and a rough read.)

So, what was wrong about David's command? Initially, I

didn't get the big deal. We have already seen that a census was a normal occurrence in the ancient world, and that God himself had commanded one. What made this one different...and a sin nonetheless?

Here's the problem: David's *intention*. With God's help, he had unified Israel and gained dominion over a vast territory. He wanted numbers to brag about. He wanted to quantify his power.

"Some scholars say that the census also marked a fundamental shift in David's foreign policy. He was moving away from diplomacy and toward military force. Readers will notice that his census counts only 'men who drew the sword.'"[79]

Five possible reasons that David's census was wrong:

1. "He was using it to number men under twenty years of age for army service, which was forbidden in God's law.
2. The census had no direct order from God.
3. David was going to use the results to tax the people more than the law allowed.
4. David was not trusting the promises of God to Abraham to make the people innumerable.
5. David was exhibiting the pride of his heart in putting confidence in the number and power of his army rather than in God.

Though they are all plausible, there is a problem with each of these proposals: no clear evidence in the text exists for any of them."[80]

It is likely that David was trying to increase his own kingly power through the census, but this was in direct contrast to a dependence on God. As we see in Deuteronomy 17, "the human kingship of Israel was to be noticeably dependent on God's divine kingship. For Israel's king to build up the same kind of power common to pagan kings was directly violating God's over-kingship."[81] It's not surprising, then, to see the angry response from God in bringing it to a quick end.

Through those lenses, it becomes obvious that the census taking is a flagrant sin. Even Joab, David's thug general who is not noted for spiritual and moral sensitivities, actually objects and thinks this is a bad idea. Thank you, Captain Obvious. (Joab was literally a caption too). But David persists. The sin-nature of the census is not explained, but students of this text are agreed that it involves a radical departure from living by faith—counting soldiers is the opposite of trusting in God.

"This particular census provides the basis for adding soldiers and assessing taxes, two primary features of depersonalized and tyrannizing state power. David's government, which is intended to represent a personal God, now moves into faceless bureaucracy. Somewhere along the line, David has become more interested in numbers than in names. The plague that follows is a dramatic rendition of what usually follows more slowly and subtly. Sin has social consequences. The evil with David was not in the 'numbering' itself, but the replacement of names by numbers."[82]

DAVID'S CHOICE OF THREE PUNISHMENTS:

- Three years of famine
- Three months of fleeing before his enemies
- Three days of plague.

David chose the third option and 70,000 men lost their lives to the plague that God sent to Israel. Do we wonder, as David did, why the Lord would punish a nation for the sin of one man? And David himself even asked God to spare the people and punish only his family.

God, of course, doesn't owe David—or any of us—an answer as to why. Perhaps it was a long overdue punishment for the other sins of Israel. Or maybe it was a reminder of what happens when a leader goes off the rails. Or maybe there was a different reason.

"Of the choices presented to David, the first two would have involved dependency upon the mercy of man: the warfare, of course, would be as severe as the enemy wanted it to be; the famine would require Israel to seek food from other nations, relying on the pity of their neighbors. Instead of relying on the mercy of any human, David chose to rely on the mercy of God—the pestilence was, after all, the most direct form of punishment from God, and in the plague they could only look to God for relief."[83]

David's sin results in a plague that kills seventy thousand people. I can't even imagine receiving that total death count as a leader. David responded by taking responsibility and praying for mercy. After his census taking, which was a complete prideful act of ambition and power, David found himself dealing with God. A different prophet, Gad, brought God's word to him (Nathan did this work on earlier occasions.) David quickly found himself back to dealing with his heart.

DAVID'S TWO PRAYERS:

1. His first prayer was one of repentance

David once again knew he had done wrong and admitted it. He accepted responsibility and interceded for those who are suffering because of his sin. We are not told how he came to this realization, but he did—and his first response to his sin was to pray. David dealt with God.

2. His second prayer was one of intercession

His second response was to pray for those who were caught in the consequences of his sin. David did not always obey God, but he always dealt with God. David was not always sensitive to God, but he always ended up calling on God. David was not always prayerful, but he always ended up praying. Oh, that I would respond in my sinful actions with both of these types of prayers.

"This final David story has, fittingly, David praying, confessing his sins and caring for the people. His prayer is personal and for the people. The psalms, so many of which are directly credited to David, remember David primarily as a person of prayer."[84]

As a road warrior, we never want painful consequences for ourselves, but we especially don't want those we lead to suffer as the result of our choices. May this be a humbling wake-up call to those in leadership that our decisions matter.

QUESTION

What potentially selfish decisions are you making in business and/or life that is dishonoring God? How could those choices affect those around you?

TODAY'S ROAD PRAYER

God, it's so easy to make decisions in a vacuum—especially on the road—that have major consequences. How often we make them without seeking counsel from You and those around us.

No matter my age or my role, may I seek You first. Then help me seek out those around me that can guide me to choose decisions that serve You and others, not solely for my own glory.

I give you THIS DAY to become a road warrior after Your own heart.

Write down the potentially selfish decisions that are in motion and can be prevented, if you take action now.

SEASON FIVE
David as a Family Man

DAVID AS A FAMILY MAN

5.1 FOOLISH

How is More Than One Wife a Good Idea?

And David took him more concubines and wives out of Jerusalem, after he was come from Hebron: and there were yet sons and daughters born to David (2 Samuel 5:13 ESV).

I've been divorced. Not all marriages last, of course, and when children are involved, it can get messy. You still have this relationship as co-parents, but the love you once had is gone. Dealing with each other through kids and child support can be more challenging than expected. It's not the path or outcome you planned, but there are still consequences and responsibilities to face.

But David, voluntarily choosing to have not just another wife at the same time, but *multiple* wives? How is that a good idea? And this was decided by the man who was known for his intelligence in war, the arts, managing people, and his faith. Only one word is fitting of this line of thinking: FOOLISH. C'mon, David!

"He collected wives as trophies. He saw spouses as a means to his pleasure, not a part of God's plan."[85]

"David didn't simply have six children…he had six children by six different wives. This polygamy was one of the dark spots in David's life that later came back to haunt him…

David had a total of twenty sons and one daughter…I want you to keep all this in mind, because David's enormous family becomes an important issue later in his life, especially after his adultery with Bathsheba. He had, along with the wives, some of whom aren't even mentioned, a number of nameless concubines. This sizable family began during his years in Hebron, where he reigned in a limited capacity for seven and a half years."[86]

Remember, the people of Israel wanted a king, someone they could see and who acted like a king. And David played this part of his kingship to the extreme in both pleasure and pain.

We also must remember that, in the era when David lived, marriages were different. People still fell in love, of course. (In 1 Samuel, Michal told her father, King Saul, that she loved David.) However, money, prestige, and politics usually played a much more influential role than love did.

"David acts like a king. He has concubines (to add to his) many wives. Now in the royal city there is a new vocabulary for a new practice. The new language and new practice appear without apology. David is well into the process of sexual politics."[87]

David's first wife was given to him as a prize for killing Goliath. Yet she only loved David until her psycho father literally was trying to kill her husband. No family dysfunction there! Michal helped David escape but turns on him immediately to protect herself by lying to her father. David is alone. Again.

Then he found the prize jewel, the Proverbs 31 woman in Abigail. Beautiful *and* intelligent? He became "that guy" who gets both in a woman. And this was the woman every guy was wishing he had as his wife. And she was all David's. Michal was gone. One man, one wife—just the way God designed it.

But it wasn't enough for our hero. He just *had* to have more. And oh, did he ever. David couldn't use the excuse of culture, even though Israel modeled having a king like everyone else. David went into this mess with eyes wide-open.

"God said there were at least three things the king of Israel must not do:

1. He must not multiply horses for himself or allow his people to return to Egypt to multiply horses.
2. He must not multiply wives for himself.
3. He must not greatly increase silver and gold for himself.

David was faithful in the first and the third; but being a man of passion, he failed in the second...The simple fact is that the passion of sex is not satisfied by a full harem of women; it is increased...His lust and polygamy secretly began to erode his integrity."[88]

Don't make David's mistake. Max Lucado puts in blunt terms. "Be fiercely loyal to one spouse. Fiercely loyal. Don't even look twice at someone else. No flirting. No teasing. No loitering at her desk or lingering in his office. Who cares if you come across as rude or a prude? You've made a promise. Keep it."[89]

Here's where this hits home for the road warrior.

ON THE ROAD, THERE ARE SPECIFIC AREAS THAT TAKE OUR EYES OFF GOD:

1. How we use our POWER on the road

It's so easy to mention our role or position...and even embellish it. Why? To make ourselves sound more appealing and attractive. The problem comes when it's with the opposite sex. You know when you play the power card, the game changes. It feels good in the moment but rarely if ever leads to something good in the long run. I've seen this too many times by men of power on the road, and all for the sake of business. They experience only the pleasure in the moment, but the pain of the future will cost tenfold.

The Challenge: Keep your power in perspective. God has allowed you to have it in the moment and is watching how you handle your power.

2. How we use our PASSIONS on the road

Almost every successful road warrior is passionate. This is what has made them successful but also vulnerable. There is nothing wrong with passion in and of itself, but rarely is it isolated.

In my life, I've enjoyed the attention of women too much. And it's been to my own detriment. I've not crossed the affair line but easily could've too many times. Here's the point: I know when I'm pushing it and enjoying the attention too much. It's selfish, and it's dishonoring to my spouse and children. If you're gregarious and inviting, know thyself. And recognize when you're using this trait for your own pleasure.

The Challenge: Keep your passion in healthy outlets. It's so easy to be too far gone before you realize how far you've gone.

3. How we use our PRIVATE TIME on the road

This is the "when no one else is around, no one is looking, and no one will know" part of the program. Too often for the spiritual road warrior, it becomes a trigger that starts us down an unhealthy place. I've met that guy and been that guy where the private time was party time for the evil one. A simple click could send me entering a downward spiral that was addictive and sinful. Oh, you know exactly what I mean.

The Challenge: Keep your private time accountable time. Especially as a spiritual road warrior, you need to have someone know how you are using your private time on the road.

How you use your power, your passions, and your private time on the road can make or break you in your quest to becoming a road warrior after God's own heart.

There's a pretty good chance you don't have multiple wives or spouses. But that's not the point here. Yes, David was wrong in this area and disobeyed God, and that left carnage in his family. The point is, David allowed the evil one a foothold in an area of weakness for our man after God's own heart. And it could've been avoided.

This dark spot in David's life should be a wake-up call for those of us abusing our power, passions, and private time on the road. Our actions may be dishonoring our spouse and/or kids, and most of all, God.

But all of this can change in a moment. Right here. Right now. May God's Holy Spirit speak in a way that you hear and respond.

QUESTION

How are you dishonoring the significant people in your life (spouse, kids, or friends) while on the road? What do you need to do differently today to change that dishonor to honor?

TODAY'S ROAD PRAYER

God, I am thankful for the power, passions, and private time the road allows me. But I also realize how quickly and easily I can use them for selfish and sinful purposes.

I want to learn from the mistakes of David in this area of accumulation that can lead me away from obeying You in every area of my life.

May I seek to honor You first on the road in this area and, as a result, honor my significant other naturally.

Reveal to me right now how my thoughts and actions need to change in this specific area so I can become a road warrior after God's own heart.

Write down how you're abusing your power, passions, and private time, and what you'll do to change it for the good today.

5.2 DESIRE

Giving into Temptation and the Cover-up

In the spring, at the time when kings go off to war, David sent Joab out with the king's men and the whole Israelite army. They destroyed the Ammonites and besieged Rabbah. But David remained in Jerusalem.

One evening David got up from his bed and walked around on the roof of the palace. From the roof he saw a woman bathing. The woman was very beautiful, and David sent someone to find out about her. The man said, "She is Bathsheba, the daughter of Eliam and the wife of Uriah the Hittite." Then David sent messengers to get her. She came to him, and he slept with her. (Now she was purifying herself from her monthly uncleanness.) Then she went back home. The woman conceived and sent word to David, saying, "I am pregnant."

So David sent this word to Joab: "Send me Uriah the Hittite." And Joab sent him to David. When Uriah came to him, David asked him how Joab was, how the soldiers were and how the war was going. Then David said to Uriah, "Go down to your house and wash your feet." So Uriah left the palace, and a gift from the king was sent after him. But Uriah slept at the entrance to the palace with all his master's servants and did not go down to his house.

David was told, "Uriah did not go home." So he asked Uriah, "Haven't you just come from a military campaign? Why didn't you go home?"

Uriah said to David, "The ark and Israel and Judah are staying in tents, and my commander Joab and my lord's men are camped in the open country. How could I go to my house to eat and drink and make love to my wife? As surely as you live, I will not do such a thing!"

Then David said to him, "Stay here one more day, and tomorrow I will send you back." So Uriah remained in Jerusalem that day and the next. At David's invitation, he ate and drank with him, and David made him drunk. But in the evening Uriah went out to sleep on his mat among his master's servants; he did not go home.

In the morning David wrote a letter to Joab and sent it with Uriah. In it he wrote, "Put Uriah out in front where the fighting is fiercest. Then withdraw from him so he will be struck down and die."

So while Joab had the city under siege, he put Uriah at a place where he knew the strongest defenders were. When the men of the city came out and fought against Joab, some of the men in David's army fell; moreover, Uriah the Hittite died.

Joab sent David a full account of the battle. He instructed the messenger: "When you have finished giving the king this account of the battle, the king's anger may flare up, and he may ask you, 'Why did you get so close to the city to fight? Didn't you know they would shoot arrows from the wall? Who killed Abimelek son of Jerub-Besheth? Didn't a woman drop an upper millstone on him from the wall, so that he died in Thebez? Why did you get so close to the wall?' If he asks you this, then say to him, 'Moreover, your servant Uriah the Hittite is dead.'"

The messenger set out, and when he arrived he told David everything Joab had sent him to say. The messenger said to David, "The men overpowered us and came out against us in the open, but we drove them back to the entrance of the city gate. Then the archers shot arrows at your servants from the wall, and some of the king's men died. Moreover, your servant Uriah the Hittite is dead."

David told the messenger, "Say this to Joab: 'Don't let this upset you; the sword devours one as well as another. Press the attack against the city and destroy it.' Say this to encourage Joab."

When Uriah's wife heard that her husband was dead, she mourned for him. After the time of mourning was over, David had her brought to his house, *and she became his wife and bore him a son. But the thing David had done displeased the Lord* (2 Samuel 11:1-27 NIV).

When we think of the life of David, we usually associate two people with him—Goliath and Bathsheba. They are permanently linked with him, but in very opposite ways.

"The two names are well established in the memory of even casual readers of the Bible. The physical forms attached to the names could hardly be more different: Goliath—the ugly, cruel giant; Bathsheba—the beautiful, gentle woman. Goliath, an evil tyrant; Bathsheba, an innocent victim. But different as Goliath and Bathsheba are in character and appearance, there is a similarity in the place they hold in David's life. Both bring him into places of testing. The giant and the woman enter David's life at contrasting times.

In the meeting with Goliath, David is young, unknown, and untested. In the meeting with Bathsheba, David is mature, well known, and thoroughly tested and tried. In the first meeting, David emerges triumphant; in the second meeting, he goes down in defeat."[90]

Considering the victory with Goliath, we are not at all prepared for this disgraceful defeat. How could this happen? How could an "innocent look" turn into an affair *and a murder*? Like most falls, bit by bit, without David even realizing it was happening.

"David is at an all-time high. He is fresh off a series of great victories on the battlefield. He has reached the peak of public admiration. He has ample money, incredible power, unquestioned authority, remarkable fame. His lifestyle looks like this—an arrow going farther and farther up into the clouds, like the sharp climb of a plane after takeoff as it increases in altitude. Farther and farther and farther up into the clouds went the life of David. And as a result, he was vulnerable.

Our most difficult times are not when things are going hard. Hard times create dependent people. You don't get proud when you're dependent on God. Survival keeps you humble. Pride happens when everything is swinging in your direction."[91]

Twelve words: "In the spring, at the time when kings go off to war." They were David's demise.

"In the evening, at the time when Christians go on the road" can be to our demise and our guilty-by-association with David's story.

The truth is that David should've been looking for a sharp right turn by "going off to war." Instead, he ended up with a smooth downward slope that became a completely different battle, one he could not and would not win. One more scroll. One more click. One more drink. One more comment.

I may be in the minority, but I believe David knew exactly what was going to happen that evening. Little was random in his life, especially within his view and control. He planned to be alone. He planned to be on the balcony. He planned to catch a peak. He planned to take it as far as he could. He knew she would be there.

Sound familiar?

You plan to have some free time in the evening on the road. You plan to open up your computer or go down to the hotel bar. You plan to click or to flirt. You plan to take it as far as you could. Just a little more each time. No harm in that, right? And nobody will ever know.

In this situation, David is not just vulnerable. He's *unaccountable*.

David was in bed, not in battle. Had he been where he belonged, with his troops, there might never have been the Bathsheba episode but more like a Joseph leave-my-coat-and-escape episode. David might have been linked with only one name and one battle: Goliath.

Our greatest battles don't usually come when we're working hard; they come when we have some leisure, when we've got time on our hands, when we're bored. We claim as road warriors that we're *always* busy, but that's not the case. We have more discretionary time than we admit to. That's when we make those fateful decisions that come back to haunt us. That's where David was—indulging himself beyond the boundaries of wisdom. He belonged in the battle; instead, he was on the balcony in a completely different battle.

I've often wondered about the backstory on David's location. I found in my research that "Eastern monarchs frequently built their bedchambers on the second story of the palace and had a door that opened onto what you and I would call a patio roof. Often it was elegantly furnished, a place to sit with his family or with his men in counsel. Situated above the public demands and away from the streets, it was secreted."[92]

I also don't believe Bathsheba is without responsibility. She had to know others were watching especially in light of the way housing was set-up in these times. Raymond Brown, in his work on David's life, suggests, "When we read this terrible story we instinctively think of the offense as David's sin, but this attractive woman cannot be entirely excused. Bathsheba was careless and foolish, lacking in the usual Hebrew modesty, or she certainly would not have washed in a place where she knew she could be overlooked. From her roof-top she would often have looked out to the royal palace and must have known that she could be seen."[93]

I believe both David and Bathsheba were at fault on this occasion, but of the two, certainly David was the aggressor. He stopped. He stared. He lusted. He sought her. He lost control of his passion. He intentionally initiated physical contact knowing full well where it would lead.

"David sent and inquired about the woman." And notice the report. "Is this not Bathsheba, the daughter of Eliam, the wife of Uriah the Hittite?" (2 Samuel 11:3 NKJV). I find that statement incredibly significant. This soft-spoken yet bold servant throws out a subtle and obvious warning of wisdom to the king.

In other words, "I know you're the boss and all, but that lady's married."

"The servant laces his information with a warning. He gives not only the woman's name but her marital status and the name of her husband. Why tell David she is married if not to caution him? And why give the husband's name unless David is familiar with it? Odds are, David knew Uriah. The servant hopes to deftly dissuade the king. But David misses the hint."[94]

I have little doubt that the servant knew exactly what David was thinking. He could see her down there. He was a man as well. He knew his master. He'd seen the harem. He'd watched David operate with women, and so he warned him as he answered him. But it doesn't even seem to register with David. C'mon, man.

Do you have that kind of person in your life? Someone who sees your behavior and offers a soft but needed warning from time-to-time?

By now David's desire for sexual pleasure with that woman was off the charts. He moved quickly, ignoring any warning and all consequences. As a result, David leverages his entourage to get her for one night of pleasure (2 Samuel 11:4 NKJV).

Now, let's be absolutely realistic here. We would be foolish to think that there was no pleasure in this encounter between David and Bathsheba. This act carried with it an enormous amount of sensual excitement. The gazing, the request, the conquest.

It's been my observation over the years that the devil never tips his hand in temptation. He shows you only the beauty, the ecstasy, the fun, the excitement, and the stimulating adventure of stolen desires. But he never tells the heavy drinker, "You're going to get a DUI on the road. Tomorrow morning there'll be a hangover. Ultimately, you'll ruin your family." Or to the lusting heart "Clicking on some porn sites is probably going to become an addiction, and it'll lead to the destruction of your marriage."

Face it, when the sin is done and all the penalties of that sin come due, the devil is nowhere to be found. He smiles as you fall…but he leaves you with no encouragement when the consequences kick in, just endless shame. He's good at that.

THERE WERE TWO SCENES TO DAVID'S NIGHT OF PLEASURE:

1. The Plan:
- The Look: view her
- The Inquiry: get her

The problem is David only planned on the 1st scene of his one-night stand ending in a fantastic finish.

But sin never seems to work that way, road warrior. For you or for King David. As a result, scene two kicks in and goes dark quickly.

2. The Panic:
- The News: she's pregnant
- The Scheme: her husband's death

Notice, David the strategist is active this entire time and goes on a "sending spree." His actions were all about control, to bring pleasure or limit consequences. He sent:

- To inquire about Bathsheba
- To get Bathsheba
- To (Joab) to bring Uriah
- Uriah home (twice)
- Uriah into battle to die
- To get Bathsheba a second time, but this time to stay[95]

"We don't like this sending, demanding David. We prefer the pastoring David, caring for the flock; the dashing David, hiding from Saul; the worshiping David, penning psalms. We aren't prepared for the David who has lost control of his self-control, who sins as he sends.

What has happened to him? Simple. Altitude sickness. He's been too high too long. The thin air has messed with his senses. He can't hear as he used to. He can't hear the warnings of the servant or the voice of his conscience. Nor can he hear his Lord. The pinnacle has dulled his ears and blinded his eyes. Did David see Bathsheba? No. He saw Bathsheba bathing. He saw Bathsheba's body and Bathsheba's curves. He saw Bathsheba, the conquest. But did he see Bathsheba, the human being? The wife of Uriah? The daughter of Israel? The creation of God? No. David had lost his vision. Too long at the top will do that to you."[96]

Are you keeping count of David's sins? Lust, adultery, hypocrisy, murder. How could a man—a man after God's own heart—fall to such a level? Hey, Jerry Judge, if you are honest about your own heart, it's not hard to understand.

"And so, the sad, dark chapter of David's fall comes to an end. Or does it? Nowhere close. The man is now trapped in a swirl of misery, which he describes in detail in Psalm 32:3–4 NIV as well as Psalm 51:3–4 NIV. Sleepless nights. Physical illness. A fever. Haunted memories. Loss of weight. Total misery. The worst: feeling so terribly alone. So many miles from God. So full of groaning and agonizing."[97]

When a messenger arrives from the battlefield, he has the news that David has been waiting to hear: "Your servant Uriah the Hittite is dead also."

Of course, that's *all* David hears. He doesn't show any remorse for the many other soldiers who also died in battle that day as a direct result of David's sin. Instead, David sends an encouraging message to Joab, and moves right to the next part of his plan.

A few days later, when Bathsheba's period of mourning for her husband ended. David took her as his wife, and she gave birth to a son (2 Samuel 11:27 NASB).

So, just one question hangs in the air:

"Why in the world did David murder Uriah? What did he gain by it?

Think about that. If Uriah had lived and come home from battle and found his wife pregnant, who would have ever connected it to David? It's doubtful she would have ever said a word. Then, after Uriah was killed, David immediately took her to the palace and married her—and it's been my observation that most adults can count to nine. So, who in the world was David hiding from?

When you act in panic, you don't think logically. In fact, you usually don't think. You react. You overlook and cover up and smear over and cloud over and deny and scheme until you find yourself in the midst of such a maze of lies that you can never escape or get the mess untangled. Until you finally face someone honest enough to say, 'You are the man!'"[98]

Meanwhile, at the end of this awful episode we read eleven simple words: "David did what was evil in the sight of the Lord" (2 Samuel 11:27 NASB). Period. In that brief statement we see the raw, open sewage of David's life.

QUESTION

If this chapter hit a little too close to home with you, what stage are you in right now—the planning stage or the panic stage?

TODAY'S ROAD PRAYER

God, it's so easy when I'm not living in sin to become Jerry Judge and not Empathetic Ed.

I so quickly forgot how easy it is to fall on the road on any given day then spend as much energy in the panic stage as I did in the planning stage.

May You soften my conscience today, right now, to see and feel whom You've put in my life to stop me in my tracks and turn to You and You alone. Not the pleasure but the peace that passes all understanding to guard my heart.

I give you THIS DAY to become a road warrior after Your own heart.

Select just one word that has been predominant in your mind as you read this chapter:

- Plan
- Panic
- Boredom
- Adventure
- Numb

5.3 PASSIVE

Angry Is All We Get Out of You After THAT Happened, Dad?

In the course of time, Amnon son of David fell in love with Tamar, the beautiful sister of Absalom son of David.

Amnon became so obsessed with his sister Tamar that he made himself ill. She was a virgin, and it seemed impossible for him to do anything to her.

Now Amnon had an adviser named Jonadab son of Shimeah, David's brother. Jonadab was a very shrewd man. He asked Amnon, "Why do you, the king's son, look so haggard morning after morning? Won't you tell me?"

Amnon said to him, "I'm in love with Tamar, my brother Absalom's sister."

"Go to bed and pretend to be ill," Jonadab said. "When your father comes to see you, say to him, 'I would like my sister Tamar to come and give me something to eat. Let her prepare the food in my sight so I may watch her and then eat it from her hand.'"

So Amnon lay down and pretended to be ill. When the king came to see him, Amnon said to him, "I would like my sister Tamar to come and make some special bread in my sight, so I may eat from her hand."

David sent word to Tamar at the palace: "Go to the house of your brother Amnon and prepare some food for him." So Tamar went to the house of her brother Amnon, who was lying down. She took some dough, kneaded it, *made the bread in his sight and baked it. Then she took the pan and served him the bread, but he refused to eat.*

"Send everyone out of here," Amnon said. So everyone left him. Then Amnon said to Tamar, "Bring the food here into my bedroom so I may eat from your hand." And Tamar took the bread she had prepared and brought it to her brother Amnon in his bedroom. But when she took it to him to eat, he grabbed her and said, "Come to bed with me, my sister."

"No, my brother!" she said to him. "Don't force me! Such a thing should not be done in Israel! Don't do this wicked thing. What about me? Where could I get rid of my disgrace? And what about you? You would be like one of the wicked fools in Israel. Please speak to the king; he will not keep me from being married to you." But he refused to listen to her, and since he was stronger than she, he raped her.

Then Amnon hated her with intense hatred. In fact, he hated her more than he had loved her. Amnon said to her, "Get up and get out!"

"No!" she said to him. "Sending me away would be a greater wrong than what you have already done to me."

But he refused to listen to her. He called his personal servant and said, "Get this woman out of my sight and bolt the door after her." So his servant put her out and bolted the door after her. She was wearing an ornate robe, for this was the kind of garment the virgin daughters of the king wore. Tamar put ashes on her head and tore the ornate robe she was wearing. She put her hands on her head and went away, weeping aloud as she went.

Her brother Absalom said to her, "Has that Amnon, your brother, been with you? Be quiet for now, my sister; he is your brother. Don't take this thing to heart." And Tamar lived in her brother Absalom's house, a desolate woman.

When King David heard all this, he was angry. And Absalom never said a word to Amnon, either good or bad; he hated Amnon because he had disgraced his sister Tamar (2 Samuel 13:1-21 NIV).

Out of all the examples of the Bible, ideal parenting is not at the top of the list. Most of the examples we learn are what *not* to do. The more I studied this story, the more I struggled with the parent in David, or lack thereof. As a result, we'll look at three angles of David as a father.

David is used twice in this particular story. Misled and duped in his own family who ultimately becomes an accomplice in some rated R for sex and violence action and drama, TMZ style.

This specific story with David's kids feels like it comes out of nowhere, but as we unpack the backstory, it's not a surprise at all.

"This is the first installment of Nathan's prophesied consequences of David's sin against Bathsheba and Uriah: 'I will raise up trouble against you from within your own house.' II Samuel 12:11 Trouble to put it midly: David's virgin daughter violated; David's firstborn son a rapist. David's violation of Bathsheba is now played out before his own eyes in his own home in Amnon's violation of Tamar; soon his murder of Uriah will be reproduced in Absalom's murder of Amnon."[99] This is sadly and painfully David's inner world imploding right before his very eyes.

While we have limited access to a full genealogical record of all David's wives, children, and concubines, we do have an intimate, unedited record of the relationship between Absalom and Amnon and Tamar. Those three were David's children, but Absalom and Tamar came from one mother; Amnon, another.

Here's the disturbing backstory. Amnon was attracted to his half-sister Tamar, the blood sister of Absalom. It was a disgraceful, disgusting kind of love. Better defined, it was incestuous lust. But how did he pull his master evil plan off? With a little help from an advisor.

The Jonadab plan is ingenious. Insert "bwa-ha-ha" sinister laughter here. First, get King David involved. With David playing a leading role, no one will suspect any foul play, least of all David himself, David, without the slightest suspicion that he is being used to further his son's raging lust, does what he is asked. Tamar is sent to Amnon. And Tamar, also unsuspecting, does what she is told. She prepares food for Amnon. But more than simple nourishment is involved—she is not just to bring in a casserole and drop it off. She prepares a meal in his presence, and the food preparation itself seems to serve as a kind of ritual of comfort, elaborate and time-consuming along with time for Amnon's lust to cook as well.

She has been depersonalized into a target for his lust. As far as Amnon is concerned, Tamar is nothing but a piece of pornography. Once she is depersonalized into a sex object, he can do whatever he wishes. (Oops. Did I just get personal?) Amnon rapes Tamar. And then, "seized with a very great loathing" (v. 15), he hates her. Amnon throws her out of the house into the street and locks the door against her. First rape, then hate.

"Amnon has violated her body; now he violates her soul. Outer and inner wounds on a grand scale. Violated Tamar now laments on a grand scale. What has taken place in the privacy of Amnon's room, Tamar proceeds to broadcast publicly through the streets of Jerusalem. She tears her beautiful virgin's robe, covers her head with ashes, and demonstrates her violation by dramatic gesture and loud weeping."[100]

How did Absalom, Tamar's brother, handle this news? Silence. Passive, at least for now. Absalom and Amnon did not speak for two years. For two full years this bitterness and hatred ate away at Absalom.

A brother hates a brother. Lust has led to rape; rape has led to hatred; and now hatred leads to the next step, which is murder.

Back to the main character of this book, the man after God's own heart. How did David handle this news?

The only place I can find in any reference to David as it relates to his daughter being violated by his son was in the text: "Now when King David heard of all these matters, he was very angry" (2 Samuel 13:21 ESV).

Ya think!? What did you do with that anger, David? Yell at the kids? Or did you swallow that anger and become passive-aggressive and take it out on everyone and everything else?

"When David learns of the rape, he is angry, but his anger does not amount to anything. Anger that is provoked by arriving at a scene like this, anger that is an outrage over the desecration of life, can become a powerful fuel for justice, for setting things right, for getting wrongdoers back on the right path and helping the wronged. But nothing comes of David's anger.

David's anemic anger leaves Amnon unpunished and Tamar ignored. But that is not the end of it, for it starts Absalom on a path of violence. But when his father fails to respond adequately, the injustice enters Absalom's soul; it seethes and rankles there. If David will not act justly, he will."[101]

Classic passivity. Incredible paternal preoccupation. His head is somewhere else. It has been for a long time. These kids have raised themselves, without the proper parental authority and discipline. And this passiveness affects them their entire adult lives. How they felt about David's passive response mattered.

How did Amnon feel about his father's passivity?

- Relieved
- Enabled
- Justified

How did Tamar feel about her father's passivity?

- Neglected
- Hopeless

How did Absalom feel about his father's passivity?

- Hatred
- Revengeful

What kind of palace did David provide physically for his umpteen wives and children? It was fabulous. Top shelf. They probably had every material thing they wanted. But money cannot buy the best things in life. Things couldn't solve the problem within the relationships of that home. Amnon raped and then hated his sister. Absalom hated his brother, and he did so for two full years. They didn't even speak. What a nightmare of a home the palace must have been! C'mon, David, be a father.

King David offered his kids everything they could possibly want when it comes to lifestyle. Except himself. A father needs to be a father in the life of his kids.

I have two older sons from a previous marriage. Over a decade later, I still mourn and regret not having them in my life on a daily basis. I still have to forgive their mother for leaving the marriage. When they're with me, every moment counts especially now in their college years. I don't want conflict. I want peace, happiness, and good memories.

I can understand the passivity of David and too often fight those overwhelming suggestions to just let things go. But I can't. There is a price as we've seen with David.

THREE NECESSARY ACTIONS TO AVOID PASSIVITY

1. INVEST: We must invest into the lives of our children when we're on the road by connecting with them through intentional, thoughtful, and creative ways. We must build these relationships so when we are home, we've continued—not paused—the relationship while we were gone.

2. GRACE: We must give ourselves grace while we're on the road and not beat ourselves up for being gone. There are creative ways to leverage the road to grow these key relationships even when we're not physically home.

3. FORGIVE: We must also forgive ourselves for past sins and have the David Complex of "who am I to correct this when I've done that?" attitude.

I hurt for David and too often mirror this side of him as a father. But I don't want the cost which motivates me to change. Today. Right now. And I hope you do as well.

QUESTION

How have you been or are currently passive in the life of your family right now, and what needs to be changed?

TODAY'S ROAD PRAYER

God, it's just so easy to let things go especially when I'm on the road. To let whoever is home take care of things. To be the hero when I come home and avoid any tension.

But this is wrong and will cause long-term consequences. I don't want to be this passive parent and want my family to experience a consistent me no matter where I am at all times.

May I be gentle to Your Spirit to change in the ways that You bring to my attention that need attention.

I give you THIS DAY to become a road warrior after Your own heart.

Write down any ways you're being passive with your family and how you can change it today.

5.4 ABSENT

Any Chance of Making an Appearance, Dad?

READ

Two years later, when Absalom's sheep shearers were at Baal Hazor near the border of Ephraim, he invited all the king's sons to come there. Absalom went to the king and said, "Your servant has had shearers come. Will the king and his attendants please join me?"

"No, my son," the king replied. "All of us should not go; we would only be a burden to you." Although Absalom urged him, he still refused to go but gave him his blessing.

Then Absalom said, "If not, please let my brother Amnon come with us."

The king asked him, "Why should he go with you?" But Absalom urged him, so he sent with him Amnon and the rest of the king's sons.

Absalom ordered his men, "Listen! When Amnon is in high spirits from drinking wine and I say to you, 'Strike Amnon down,' then kill him. Don't be afraid. Haven't I given you this order? Be strong and brave.'" So Absalom's men did to Amnon what Absalom had ordered. Then all the king's sons got up, mounted their mules and fled.

While they were on their way, the report came to David: "Absalom has struck down all the king's sons; not one of them is left." The king stood up, tore his clothes and lay down on the ground; and all his attendants stood by with their clothes torn.

But Jonadab son of Shimeah, David's brother, said, "My lord should

169

not think that they killed all the princes; only Amnon is dead. This has been Absalom's express intention ever since the day Amnon raped his sister Tamar. My lord the king should not be concerned about the report that all the king's sons are dead. Only Amnon is dead."

Meanwhile, Absalom had fled.

Now the man standing watch looked up and saw many people on the road west of him, coming down the side of the hill. The watchman went and told the king, "I see men in the direction of Horonaim, on the side of the hill."

Jonadab said to the king, "See, the king's sons have come; it has happened just as your servant said." As he finished speaking, the king's sons came in, wailing loudly. The king, too, and all his attendants wept very bitterly.

Absalom fled and went to Talmai son of Ammihud, the king of Geshur. But King David mourned many days for his son. After Absalom fled and went to Geshur, he stayed there three years. And King David longed to go to Absalom, for he was consoled concerning Amnon's death (2 Samuel 13:23–39 NIV).

The king said to Joab, "Very well, I will do it. Go, bring back the young man Absalom."

Then Joab went to Geshur and brought Absalom back to Jerusalem. But the king said, "He must go to his own house; he must not see my face." So Absalom went to his own house and did not see the face of the king.

In all Israel there was not a man so highly praised for his handsome appearance as Absalom. From the top of his head to the sole of his foot there was no blemish in him.

Three sons and a daughter were born to Absalom. His daughter's name was Tamar, and she became a beautiful woman.

Absalom lived two years in Jerusalem without seeing the king's face. Then Absalom sent for Joab in order to send him to the king, but Joab refused to come to him. So he sent a second time, but he refused to come. Then he said to his servants, "Look, Joab's field is next to mine, and he has barley there. Go and set it on fire." So Absalom's servants set the field on fire.

Then Joab did go to Absalom's house, and he said to him, "Why have your servants set my field on fire?"

Absalom said to Joab, "Look, I sent word to you and said, 'Come here so I can send you to the king to ask, "Why have I come from Geshur? It would be better for me if I were still there!"' Now then, I want to see the king's face, and if I am guilty of anything, let him put me to death."

So Joab went to the king and told him this. Then the king summoned Absalom, and he came in and bowed down with his face to the ground before the king. And the king kissed Absalom (2 Samuel 14:21,23-25,27-33 NIV).

REFLECT

It's one of the most difficult conversations I hear all too often from road warrior fathers. A child, usually in their teens, turns to their road warrior parent and says, "Who are you to tell me what to do when you're hardly ever home."

Those words hurt my heart, and it's not even coming from my kid. I feel the pain in the road warrior who's so vulnerably sharing their deepest wound. Not being present often leads to becoming passive. When you are home, the last thing you want is to be always getting on your kids.

David was passive on how he handled (or did not handle) Amnon, his eldest son, and his horrible crime of passion. But at least he was angry.

How he handled Absalom, though, after this situation was with complete silence—he was absent. Nowhere to be found. Exit, stage left. Poof, like the guy who doesn't want to pick up the check on the road.

There are not one, but two scenes where David played the absent father role in the life of Absalom. One time it lasts two years, which seems unrealistic. However, the second time lasted twice as long. C'mon, David. How do you not learn from the first time?! And you had an absent father as well.

Alexander Whyte writes in his *Dictionary of Bible Characters*:

> *"Polygamy is just Greek for a dunghill. David trampled down the first and the best law of nature in his palace in Jerusalem, and for his trouble he spent all his after-days in a hell upon earth. David's palace was a perfect pandemonium of suspicion, and intrigue, and jealousy, and hatred—all breaking out, now into incest and now murder. And it was in such a household, that Absalom, David's third son by his third wife, was brought up.*
>
> *A little ring of jealous and scheming parasites, all hateful and hating one another, collected around each one of David's wives. And it was in one of the worst of those wicked little rings that Absalom grew up and got his education.*
>
> *And the result? After two long years Absalom carries out his deceptive plan. Absalom is quite a guy, and he plays his father for a fool. He suggests a plan where all of his brothers would go to shear sheep together."* [102]

"Absalom uses his father to get Amnon to the feast where he will be killed. (Do we catch an echo here of Amnon using this same father to get Tamar to make him a meal so he could rape her?) We are not used to seeing David 'used.' We are used to seeing David take the initiative in prayer and action, leading Israel decisively. But no longer. Absalom has moved into the power vacuum left by David's failure to execute justice, his failure to 'act like a king.'" [103]

Now, if David had been on top of things in his own household, he would have known that Absalom had not spoken to Amnon for two years. Two long, painful, absent years. He would also have been aware of the hatred brewing among his children. You've got to be rather thick as a father not to know that a son isn't speaking to another son for two years. And talk about lack of control.

"Absalom's long-developed vengeance is quickly executed: He

waits until the sheep-shearing celebration is well under way, all the brothers having a good time eating and drinking, enjoying hangout time that the party provides. It's easy to imagine this large family of brothers and half-brothers making the most of this occasion to catch up on family gossip."[104]

When Absalom patiently waited for Amnon to be sufficiently drunk, he signaled his servants to kill him. Imagine holding that killer job? The murder is a bombshell. In the confusion, all the brothers quite naturally assumed that they also are marked for assassination and ran for their lives. Literally.

"As his brothers are on the run, unnecessarily as it turns out, Absalom runs for his life. He has no assurance that his father will be as lenient with him as he was with Amnon, and he does not hang around to find out: Absalom fled to the east, across the Jordan River to his maternal grandparents. His grandfather Talmai was king of the small country of Geshur. His mother, Maacah, had grown up there; Absalom will spend the next three years in asylum with his grandparents."[105] There, he licked his wounds and set up his plan later on to lead a revolt against his daddy.

"David has lost touch with what is essential to his life: Matters of affection and matters of justice are all tangled and muddled right now in the person of this son. Absalom is stuck in exile; David is stuck in loneliness."[106]

Finally, the father wound David had created in Absalom was enough. No matter how long, no matter how awkward and painful, the son needed to see his Dad. He has had enough of his absent father.

Absalom was brought back to his hometown, but his own Dad didn't want to see him. What? You bring him back from his grandparent's house to ignore him again?

Absalom's passivity he learned from his father was now long gone, this flight had definitely left the gate and he took action to get someone's—anyone's—attention. He burned down Joab's barns in hopes of getting an audience with one of the only men who can make things happen and quickly.

Absalom finally saw his father, four years after he used him to kill his brother. Instead of the prodigal son return and party, his very own son entered like everyone else, bowed, and "the king" kissed him. Notice that Absalom was not kissed by *his father* or *by David*, he was kissed by "the king." In a single verse, David is referred to as "the king" three times.

Given what we will see later in David's mourning for Absalom, this scene suggests not a lack of love but something worse—a refusal to love. Oh, how that hurts just reading those words.

"But the kiss comes too late. It has been far too long in coming. By now Absalom has changed his identity; he is no longer David's son, longing to be received by his father. Now he is David's rival, ambitious to replace his father. Was David even aware of this change in his own son's heart?"[107]

Now it becomes obvious: David's pardon of Absalom was impersonal; his forgiveness was a judicial act, not a fatherly embrace. He let Absalom return to his own city and provided him with a place to live but did not greet him by name. Nor will he permit Absalom into his presence—not so much as a look.

"Sin feeds on sin. The rape of Tamar feeds the murder of Amnon feeds the hardheartedness of David. Absalom responded to Amnon's sin by sinning. Now David responds to Absalom's sin by sinning. Absalom got rid of Amnon by killing him. David gets rid of Absalom by shunning him. David lost his son Amnon because of the sin of Absalom. David loses his son Absalom by his own sin."[108]

David turned hard on Absalom, and we're not made aware of his reasons. Did he think that what he was doing is good for Absalom, punishing him until he feels the full weight of responsibility and pain for the murder?

"Whatever line David is using to rationalize his position, underneath there is a bedrock refusal to forgive, a withholding of grace, a denial of mercy."[109] Absence became the easiest way for David to deal with his son.

There were three monumental sins of David's life at this point:

1.

1. Adultery with Bathsheba
2. Murder of her husband, Uriah
3. Rejection of Absalom

The third sin was the most inexcusable, and the one for which he would pay the highest price. "The rejection of Absalom is a steady, determined refusal to give his son what God has given David himself."[110]

Absalom spends two years plotting the murder of his brother and waiting for the right opportunity; he spends four years preparing to kill his father. Who does that?

Worse yet, who created the environment for this to even happen?

ABSENT FATHER:

- Inability to reconcile with his son
- Absalom's extreme attempts to get his father's attention (burning of Joab's farm)
- Cold, obligatory reunion
- Shunned his son again for years

This story in the family life of King David is disturbing, and there's no other way to describe it. This type of family stain doesn't "just happen." It was allowed to develop over time into extreme dysfunction and decay.

QUESTION

In what ways are you absent right now with any of your children? If so, how can you change that absence today?

TODAY'S ROAD PRAYER

God, it's so easy of accusing David with the depth of his absence as a father in the life of his kids and miss ways that we're absent in our own family.

My physical absence is obvious in this very moment which I know affects my family. May I choose to be a Connect-In Guy or Connect-In Girl not a Check-In Guy or Check-In Girl. Help me seek for intentional, thoughtful, and creative ways to stay present in the life of those that matter back home.

May I listen to the moments where You prompt me to connect with my family on the road.

I give you THIS DAY to become a road warrior after Your own heart.

Write down any ways you're being absent with your family and how you can change it today.

5.5 INCONSISTENT

Do You Have Any Idea What You're Showing Me, Dad?

Fathers, don't frustrate your children with no-win scenarios. Take them by the hand and lead them in the way of the Master (Ephesians 6:4 MSG).

One of my father's many quotes throughout his lifetime was "Son, you can learn something from anything. And oftentimes, it's what *not* to do."

This quote could not be more applicable than with David. There are so many positives in the life of David. But this man, as a father, is definitely in the "what not to do" part of the life lesson:

- Many wives
- Many concubines
- Adultery
- Deception
- Murder

- Passiveness
- Absence

As we've seen, the Bible does not pull punches in this part of David's life regarding his family. It does not try to excuse or pardon him in any way but leaves us to observe and learn from both the private and personal areas of this Bible character. We have a rare glimpse at multiple stories from different children. As a result, we've seen the passive and absent side of David as a father. Now we'll drill down on his parental inconsistency.

As road warriors, most people only see the solo artist, you, and only in the way you allow them to see you. The choice is yours whether you share the private and personal side of your family. Maybe we don't for the very reason that it's private and personal. Often, it's a timing play. Other times, there's a level of guilt and regret for this passive, absent, and inconsistent part of our lives.

I can only imagine the regret at the end of David's life in this area of his story. We can all learn from David, though, and correct what needs correction today. Right now.

The reality is whatever sin you've done or are currently doing, or however you've been as a parent, be encouraged that David's failure was far worse. And it was far more public, damaging, and extreme in the consequences.

My fourth child has three words that he often says to me. I dread hearing them but need to heed them:

"But Dad, you…"

Call it disrespect, defensive, or confrontational. The truth is he's calling out my inconsistencies. He's a challenger by nature and doesn't have a problem shedding light on what is obvious and wrong to him. It's hard to hear, but truth is truth no matter who said it or how it is said.

FOUR INCONSISTENT AREAS OF THIS SEASON OF DAVID'S LIFE AS A FAMILY MAN

1. Women

David was a man of passion, and he proved it with his many wives and concubines. Women were more of a conquest and power play in his life. Whether it was the accumulation of women or acts of adultery, women were a downfall in the life of David.

We don't see his leadership in this area as a warrior or leader. This was the time to lead, especially with the literal army of women and children under his leadership.

What did this blaring area of inconsistencies show his children? "Yeah, but you..." We know it affected his son Solomon, who accumulated over 700 wives and more concubines. Where did he learn that example?

Depending on your home life with your spouse (if married), this may hit home for most men on the road. Too many married men have wrecked their marriage or at least iced it out by their unfaithfulness on the road. Whether it's a road mistress, one-night stands, strip clubs, or flirting way too much, women are a downfall for many a male road warrior.

But I've also sadly seen too many women leverage and push this area as well. They enjoy the attention way too much, knowing they'll get whatever they want and as much as they want.

The point is "you know who you are," and if your heart is racing and conscience is screaming, it's the Holy Spirit trying to get your attention and convict you with these words.

Lesson to Learn: Faithfulness. David was unfaithful to God with the accumulation of women and unfaithful to those he had.

2. Deception

This was evident in the Bathsheba episode, but it didn't start there. We saw deception when David lied to Ahimelech the Priest, in Gath, etc. He had this side of him especially when he felt afraid, angry, and alone.

But he also showed this side to his kids. We don't know the exact ages of all of David's children, but we do know the order. All the ones older than Solomon sadly had first class seats to the drama of the adultery, cover-up, marriage, death of the child from Bathsheba, and the eventual birth of Solomon.

There are so many stories of the British royal family and the pressure, the cover-ups, the spin to "protect the family," that I can assume what it was like back in the time of David and his family. Those on the inside of the royal families know the truth, though. They see everything...especially the kids.

I can only speculate the inconsistencies David's kids witnessed through the entire real-life airing of *David and Bathsheba*.

It just seems so careless, so selfish, so wrong. But I wonder if we're deceiving those back home, especially our kids, by inconsistent actions from us on the road? Do we lead them to believe we're someone we're not? Would they feel deceived if they saw the Real You on the road?

Lesson to Learn: Truth. I was once told that you could have a lousy memory if you tell the truth because you don't have to remember any lies.

3. Abuse of Power

When David wanted something, he got it no matter how it looked or who he had to use. It's hard to accept David using people for his own benefit, but he did, and there were little eyes watching too.

Think about the Bathsheba saga. The endless sending of people to do what he wanted for his selfish gain. Countless times David was even warned, which meant they knew David was doing the wrong thing. But David the king abused his power to get what he wanted over and over.

I have a hard time with this David, yet I am him more often than I want to be. I have abused my power because "I'm in charge." I think, *I've earned this right no matter who it affects or hurts. They'll get over it.*

But it comes down to one revealing word: *entitlement*.

That potent word means "the belief that one is inherently deserving of privileges or special treatment." Did you catch that? A belief. And inherently deserving of privileges or special treatment. I do that all the time on the road, and my crown is sold separately.

The sad reality is, I do pull out my pretend road crown when I need to:

- My flight status
- My hotel status
- My rental car status

And all too often it's solely for my convenience. It uses people. It's all about me and abusing whatever power I have in my possession.

Lesson to Learn: Serving. It's difficult to abuse your power when you're seeking to serve those around you.

4. Negligence

This is the area that we see had the greatest damage to David's kids. The reality is that he just wasn't present and active in the life of his children. Maybe this stems back to his childhood and being the runt of the pack. He was shown this as a son but still had a choice to correct the sins of his father.

Not only did he avoid self-correction, though, he neglected his children to the utter extreme. Their lives were dramatically affected for the worse. How?

- Amnon rapes his sister and goes unpunished.
- Tamar is left scarred, lonely, and disregarded.
- Absalom becomes a murderer, conspirator, and manipulator.
- Solomon in all his wisdom still becomes a pleasure seeker and ends up losing his way with God.

Neglect is sneaky. It doesn't look like a deadly sin with its passivity, but the damage is paramount. Just look at the lives of David's kids and tell me otherwise. The reality is: doing nothing is doing something (another infamous quote from my late father.)

I have no doubt that if you asked any of David's kids if they wanted their father to be more active in their lives, they would quickly and definitively agree, yes!

Lesson to Learn: Responsibility. Negligence cannot co-exist with a responsible person, especially a father in the life of his children.

This confusing, disappointing, and rather horrifying season of David's life has come to a close, but it may be ongoing for you. There are so many lessons to learn from the life of David as a Family Man, even if every single one is what *not* to do. May you still learn from this dark and painful season of David's life in your desire to become a road warrior after God's own heart.

QUESTION

Where are you inconsistent in your life right now? Is it with those of the opposite sex, deception, abuse of power, negligence, or some other area?

TODAY'S ROAD PRAYER

God, often my only consistency is being inconsistent. And as someone on the road, I can and need to be more consistent. I so easily justify my inconsistency with my busy schedule and, sadly, with my sense of entitlement.

I also want, expect, and demand others to be consistent when all the while, I find myself being inconsistent. This is especially true in the areas that matter most. This needs to change.

Bring to my mind the areas where I am inconsistent and give me the discernment and strength to make the changes.

I give you THIS DAY to become a road warrior after Your own heart.

Write down any ways you're being inconsistent in your life and how you can become more consistent today.

SEASON SIX

David as a Legacy

DAVID AS A LEGACY

6.1 CALCULATED
Hostile Takeover from Within

In the course of time, Absalom provided himself with a chariot and horses and with fifty men to run ahead of him. He would get up early and stand by the side of the road leading to the city gate. Whenever anyone came with a complaint to be placed before the king for a decision, Absalom would call out to him, "What town are you from?" He would answer, "Your servant is from one of the tribes of Israel." Then Absalom would say to him, "Look, your claims are valid and proper, but there is no representative of the king to hear you." And Absalom would add, "If only I were appointed judge in the land! Then everyone who has a complaint or case could come to me and I would see that they receive justice."

Also, whenever anyone approached him to bow down before him, Absalom would reach out his hand, take hold of him and kiss him. Absalom behaved in this way toward all the Israelites who came to the king asking for justice, and so he stole the hearts of the people of Israel.

At the end of four years, Absalom said to the king, "Let me go to Hebron and fulfill a vow I made to the Lord. While your servant was living at Geshur in Aram, I made this vow: 'If the Lord takes me back to Jerusalem, I will worship the Lord in Hebron.'"

The king said to him, "Go in peace." So he went to Hebron.

Then Absalom sent secret messengers throughout the tribes of Israel to say, "As soon as you hear the sound of the trumpets, then say, 'Absalom is king in Hebron.'" Two hundred men from Jerusalem had accompanied Absalom. They had been invited as guests and went quite innocently, knowing nothing about the matter. While Absalom was offering sacrifices, he also sent for Ahithophel the Gilonite, David's counselor, to come from Giloh, his hometown. And so the conspiracy gained strength, and Absalom's following kept on increasing (2 Samuel 15:1-10 NIV).

The king answered, "I will do whatever seems best to you."

So the king stood beside the gate while all his men marched out in units of hundreds and of thousands. The king commanded Joab, Abishai and Ittai, "Be gentle with the young man Absalom for my sake." And all the troops heard the king giving orders concerning Absalom to each of the commanders.

Now Absalom happened to meet David's men. He was riding his mule, and as the mule went under the thick branches of a large oak, Absalom's hair got caught in the tree. He was left hanging in midair, while the mule he was riding kept on going.

When one of the men saw what had happened, he told Joab, "I just saw Absalom hanging in an oak tree."

Joab said to the man who had told him this, "What! You saw him? Why didn't you strike him to the ground right there? Then I would have had to give you ten shekels of silver and a warrior's belt."

But the man replied, "Even if a thousand shekels were weighed out into my hands, I would not lay a hand on the king's son. In our hearing the king commanded you and Abishai and Ittai, 'Protect the young man Absalom for my sake. And if I had put my life in jeopardy—and nothing is hidden from the king—you would have kept your distance from me.'"

Joab said, "I'm not going to wait like this for you." So he took three javelins in his hand and plunged them into Absalom's heart while Absalom was still alive in the oak tree. And ten of Joab's armor-bearers surrounded Absalom, struck him and killed him.

The king was shaken. He went up to the room over the gateway and wept. As he went, he said: "O my son Absalom! My son, my son Absalom! If only I had died instead of you—O Absalom, my son, my son!" (2 Samuel 18:4,9-15, 32-33 NIV).

Absalom. Handsome, charming, motivated, cunning, and manipulative. Sound familiar? Like father, like son, in so many aspects.

How did we get to this point in the story? In the last season, we saw David's own family impacted by rape and murder. Now an internal, calculated takeover of the throne takes center stage.

A trusted advisor of Absalom named Ahithophel had a plan for Absalom: have intercourse with your father's concubines to make sure that all of Israel knows that you are an offense to your father and to confirm the resolution of your followers (2 Samuel 16:21 NEB). Come again? That was the plan? You should read your Bible, man. Wild stories.

The whole point of the plan was for Absalom to take his pleasure with David's ten concubines in a public place where all his subjects would be able to watch. (Hey David, how about not having concubines in the first place?)

A pavilion was erected on the roof of the royal palace. Don't miss the location. It's the same place, ironically, where David had first spotted Bathsheba. Who said little eyes don't know what's going on in their own house? Each one of the concubines were then escorted to the pavilion to have sex with Absalom.

"The public spectacle depicted in the Bible can be seen as yet another lurid episode in the soap opera that King David's life so often resembled. But is also evidence of the moral example (or lack thereof) that David had set for his sons. For example, David's sexual conquest of Bathsheba may have led Amnon to believe that he could take his half-sister, Tamar, for his own pleasure without consequence. The fact that the rape of Tamar went unpunished by David prompted Absalom to take revenge against Amnon. And David's apparent weakness and lack of resolve encouraged Absalom to go into open rebellion against his father."[111]

I don't know about you, but the very idea of my own son making a hostile takeover of the family business is disturbing. It breaks my heart just thinking through it. But the saddest part of the whole story in David's situation was that the hostile takeover was completely avoidable.

David had given Absalom nothing but time and motive for what he's about to do, which allowed for ample resentment and the calculation on how to pull this off. Absalom used everything in his character and skill to steal the hearts of his father's people. He, if anyone, knew they'd been neglected in his father's later years of leadership, and he knew exactly how that feels. Not surprising that he chose that specific card to play, not violence but vigilance. In a word: calculated.

Absalom listened to the problems of David's people, and this prince swung the vote to his side, one-by-one and day-by-day. So subtle, so simple, so divisive. Brilliant and enabled, impressive and scary.

The Bible doesn't give us insight into how David viewed what Absalom was doing. He had to have known because this went on for years. Did he appreciate the help? Did he assume Absalom had a change of heart and wanted to serve his dad?

Likely, it is just another case of David as a passive, absent, and inconsistent father. This time, however, it was affecting his legacy. What was David's counsel telling him? If they were advising him, was he listening? So many questions and only assumptions.

When we don't agree with leadership, especially the older guard who may not be paying attention or caring, it's easy to try to undercut their authority with actions that may appear altruistic but are actually narcissistic. In this moment in your career, do you resonate more with Absalom or David? Maybe both, on any given road trip? Be honest. There's enough here to learn from both characters.

Absalom's "winning the hearts of the people" was only phase one of his master evil plan and a means to an end. He wanted the kingdom, and not because he was next in line after bumping off his big brother. Nor did he want to wait around for Dad to die either.

Absalom felt like he'd waited long enough and was justified to declare himself king.

This wasn't the first time this happened, and David learned something along the way by not taking matters into his own hands. Remember, David knew a thing or two about being a fugitive and making choices that had severe consequences. He hadn't forgotten the fate of the high priest at Nob, all of the other priests, and the entire village at Nob.

But this time was different. It wasn't a psychotic foreign king but David's very own son trying to take his kingdom, and Absalom's very own father loaded him with motive. Years of neglect were paying their consequence with a price a father would never want to pay.

David was sent a life-saving alert that Absalom was coming into town looking to pick a fight with Dad, so David voluntarily left his kingdom behind with everyone who sides with him. Pause for a moment and just absorb this pending scene: those feelings of confusion, anger, and defeat for all involved, especially for a father being run out of town by his son. This was not in the original legacy brochure.

David's explanation: "If I find favor in the Lord's eyes, God will bring me back and I'm not taking matters in my own hands. Let Him do to me whatever seems good to Him."

My man. Now that's the David we remember, as a man after God's own heart. It's been a long time since we've seen that, David. I'm glad he's finally back!

Can you relate? Were you known as that guy or that girl in days of old, but now you're this guy or this girl? If so, David's decision this late in his life, after so many severe consequences, should give you hope and strength to become that person again.

David never thought he was above the law. He was "a king" not "the King."

David chose not to abandon God even though it looked and felt like God had abandoned him...at least in the moment.

David's faith came back out, and he remembered this critical truth: God put me in place and will choose when, and how, and where I am replaced.[112] This decision led to David needing to take action, finally. He gave strict orders to Joab, his commander of the army, and was crystal clear with his wishes: "Be gentle with the young man Absalom for my sake."

But Joab had enough of David's passiveness, especially with a reckless, rogue son willing to do whatever it takes to bring down his father. This would definitely not happen under Joab's watch.

As fate had it, Absalom's Sampson-like hair was caught in the forest and he was left for dead, well, almost. Joab, the protector and enemy-killer, seized the moment—and the kingdom—for David. So much for "being gentle with the young man." Joab took three javelins (like one wasn't enough) to end this senseless internal battle for David's throne.

Yet, David mourned and mourned when he hears the news. His third son (the firstborn of Bathsheba from adultery, Amnon the eldest, and now Absalom) was dead, and the grief of David was all-consuming. He didn't see the reality that his kingdom was back in his control, and he could go back home with no more threats. He only saw the loss. The loss of moments he'd missed in his sons lives because of his passiveness, absence, and inconsistencies.[113]

At this time of celebration, David's failure in his family overpowered any joy and relief. And why? The cost of the victory was too high, and it was a failure that didn't need to happen in the first place.

I struggle with these later years of King David because he started so strong. So close to hearing God and that still small voice. Yet his legacy is allowed to continue only through the end of the rebellion of one of his own kids. I cannot even begin to fathom the guilt, regret, and shame that David experienced in these later years. But Nathan prophesied that because of his sin, David's family and kingdom would be ripped apart.

I don't want any part of this story for my legacy. I want to learn from this tragic story to make course corrections in my life right now. And I hope you do too.

Your legacy doesn't begin when you get to the later years in your life. David's decisions, years and years earlier, directly affected his legacy.

Decades of being passive, absent, and inconsistent as a father were paying life-altering consequences, ones that most road warriors can't even fathom. Are there choices that we're making today that could lead to unfathomable consequences within our own kingdom?

This story was a wake-up call for me, once I really thought through the ramifications of a husband and father not focused on his spouse and family. Just because I don't see any immediate consequences, it doesn't mean damage is not being done to and in the lives of those that should matter most to me back home.

Yes, King David did get his kingdom back. But Father David paid the ultimate price in losing yet another son. And what is a family kingdom with yet another loss, especially from a father who doesn't seem to be learning his lesson?

But you can.

You can start guarding your kingdom today. You can stop any damage—whether directly or indirectly—in your family kingdom. You can mitigate any rebellions and attempted overthrows by becoming a road warrior after God's own heart.

QUESTION

What are you doing right now as a spouse and/or parent that is compromising your kingdom? Is it a secret sin? Passivity? Poor example?

TODAY'S ROAD PRAYER

God, this is a tough story to read and even a tougher story to apply to our own lives. For those of us who are spouses and/or parents, may we truly feel the depth of David's loss to shake us into changing our heart and changing our ways.

You give us these difficult stories to allow us to internalize them and learn from them. Through these stories, I can listen to your still small voice and honor You by taking care of my own family kingdom.

May I make changes now to avoid future pain that is unnecessary and avoidable.

I give you THIS DAY to become a road warrior after Your own heart.

Write down the main area that has, is, or could compromise your kingdom God has given you to oversee.

6.2 DECISION

Choosing Between Two Sons

The king then took an oath: "As surely as the Lord lives, who has delivered me out of every trouble, I will surely carry out this very day what I swore to you by the Lord, the God of Israel: Solomon your son shall be king after me, and he will sit on my throne in my place" (1 Kings 1:29-30 NIV).

King David somehow survived the attempted hostile takeover of his kingdom. Even though he didn't lose his kingdom, he still lost.

At this point, David has lost three sons: Amnon, Absalom, and the nameless child that Bathsheba bore. But a new crisis developed—which of the remaining sons would succeed David on the throne? Two sons campaigned for that position: David's eldest surviving son, Adonijah, and the later son of Bathsheba, Solomon.

"The wishes of the dying king would be crucial in determining which one of them would occupy it when their father died. The very idea of dynastic succession was something wholly new in ancient Israel, and no law or custom was available to resolve the conflicting claims or Adonijah and Solomon."[114]

Adonijah seemed the obvious choice. Not only was he the oldest, but he was handsome like his brother Absalom. Even better, he hadn't disobeyed his father like Absalom had…at least up until this point. This story sounds incredibly similar to the prodigal son and his other brother written hundreds of years later. The non-troublesome son shows up in the story in a troubling way.

Adonijah became like his deceased brother by acting like a king, even without a crown. Everywhere he went, he had an entourage. He had a showoff ceremony where Solomon was somehow left off the guest list. Understandable logistical error.

"As the old king rested in his royal bedchamber, Adonijah hurried through the corridors of the palace, lobbying the king's cabinet and lining up allies in what promised to be a battle for the throne. Joab, David's ever-ruthless but ever-faithful general, sided with Adonijah, and so did Abiathar, the high priest who had survived Saul's slaughter of the priests of Nob and remained loyal to David every since."[115]

Solomon was just as effective in his campaigning, though a bit less aggressive than Adonijah. Solomon was able to secure support from Zadok, the other high priest, Nathan the Prophet, and Benaiah, commander of the palace guard. Most significantly, Solomon had the loyalty of the most influential person in King David's life—Bathsheba.

Nathan the Prophet became aware of the self-imposed crowning of Adonijah, brother and now enemy, and he let Bathsheba know. In fact, he urged her to talk to David immediately for her own protection along with Solomon.

To this point, we only know of two recorded but life-altering words from Bathsheba: "I'm pregnant." But this next recording of her words is just as powerful and life-altering for her future as well.

The final encounter between David and Bathsheba was charged with both political and sexual tension, a fitting note on which to end the life story of David. Bathsheba entered the royal bed chamber, ironically where she'd met and had adulterous sex with David. There she spotted the young woman, Abishag, who was brought in to keep David warm on his deathbed. Despite Abishag being drop-dead gorgeous (sorry, poor choice of words,) the old queen showed no lack of confidence in her own influence over David. Bathsheba simply ignored the hot chick (yes, bad pun intended) and stated her concern to David.

Bathsheba was articulate, specific, and crystal clear on what she was asking of the king and her dying husband. David heard and more importantly agreed with her. From her detailed story, David's body heated up and he responded, "As the LORD lives, who has redeemed my soul out of every adversity, as I swore to you by the LORD, the God of Israel, saying, 'Solomon your son shall reign after me, and he shall sit on my throne in my place,' even so will I do this day." (1 Kings 1:29-30 ESV). David then had his men act swiftly since time was of the essence.

"Solomon's anointment was vastly grander than his father's. David, of course had been a shepherd boy when he was called from the fields and secretly anointed by Samuel, with only his father and brothers as witnesses. By contrast, Solomon was attended by an honor guard of soldiers, was anointed by Nathan the Prophet and Zadok the High Priest, and was surrounded by a vast crowd."[116]

I wonder what that moment was like for David. So different from his anointing and path to the crown. He had to be relieved as David the king for his legacy in his public kingdom. But he also had to be concerned as David the father for his legacy in his private kingdom as a father.

In the contest for the throne, one son had to lose…and he would lose more than the kingdom, he would eventually lose his life. It didn't have to be this way. Or did it? What could David the father have done differently with Adonijah? He had lost Amnon, the eldest in one of the most horrific stories in the Bible. He then lost Absalom when he had more than enough time to reconcile that relationship, especially when Absalom wanted peace with his father.

But Adonijah was seemingly there all along. Maybe his feelings of neglect and being a no-name (which his father knew all about in his own life) came out in this passive-aggressive way to finally make a name for himself. His father was obviously not doing anything about it, so why not become the new self-proclaimed king a little early since his father was on the way out?

Oh, how this decision between two sons could've been handled so differently. What if David the king and David the father had become one to have a conversation with both of his younger sons, Adonijah and Solomon, about what would happen next?

But that would've taken a different David the father, the one from his early days of being a man after God's own heart. The David who sought and listened to God. The David who had a conscience that was so soft, he put aside emotion and opportunity to honor the true King.

I so want David's legacy to look differently. I want it to be the example we can follow step-by-step on how to end your life as a husband and father that can be modeled.

But it's just not that way. It's actually closer to real life, and that's what makes the Bible and the story of David so compelling. Real people who are selfish, sinful, and prideful who struggle with guilt, shame, and regret.

THREE LESSONS LEARNED:

1. Our time matters more than we think

As a military leader, David was gone a ton but was still home. He could've given more time to his children, especially in light of ultimately giving his kingdom to one of them one day. Yes, we're gone as road warriors, but this should make the time we are home all the more valuable and impactful. Our family wants, needs, and deserves the thing only we can give to them: our time.

2. Our words mean more than we think

David's passiveness minimized the power of his words. He obviously had them in his psalms, but they needed to be used in the life of his family. We can leverage the road to speak into the lives of our kids to prepare them for life-changing events later in their lives. Use the road time to tell your family the words they need and long to hear. They will hear them all the more when you're away on the road.

3. Our example matters more than we think

If there had to be one over-arching regret for David, it had to be the example he set for his children. He did not model the same leadership in his home as he did with his conquests. He obviously had it in him, and this story could've ended differently if he was consistent in every area of his life. Little eyes are watching whether we realize it or want them to, so our example is critical.

The longer David avoided making the seemingly right decisions in his family, the harder it was for him to make a mid-course correction. Sadly for all involved, it never happened. And when we don't make the right decisions, many suffer—and usually long after we're gone.

But you can make these changes in your own life, even while you're on the road right now. No more passivity, absence, inconsistency, and poor examples. Legacy thinking begins today, not just when we're older.

May this be a wake-up call to you in this very moment to start changing your legacy today.

 **RESPOND**

QUESTION

After this reading, what is God stirring in your heart right now that needs to change to strengthen your own legacy?

TODAY'S ROAD PRAYER

God, thinking about legacy doesn't feel urgent and isn't easy, especially if I've made poor decisions in my life that have affected others. It's easy to avoid thinking about the future and how I will be remembered. It is even easier to numb these thoughts and feelings with quick fixes that distract us and allow us to escape from reality.

But You want us to think and feel all of it right now. May I allow your still small voice to prompt my heart to sit in this moment and hear from You. Help me to truly think about my legacy through Your eyes.

I give you THIS DAY to become a road warrior after Your own heart.

Write down what God stirred in your heart about your legacy right now and any changes you can begin to make today.

6.3 EVEN THOUGH
When Your Dreams and Plans Can't Come True

Even though the fig trees have no fruit and no grapes grow on the vines,
   Even though the olive crop fails and the fields produce no grain,
   Even though the sheep all die and the cattle stalls are empty,
   I will still be joyful and glad, because the Lord God is my Savior (Habakkuk 3:17-18 GNT).

I've made selfish, damaging choices that have and will continue to alter my life and those closest to me. I have regrets that, at a moment's notice, can take me down and paralyze me if I give the evil one just an ounce of attention. On way too many occasions, the evil one has used those past regrets (although forgiven by God) to haunt me. This is still an area of healing for me, especially as we consider the legacy in our own lives. Having a trusted counselor like Dr. Nick Howard, who wrote the foreword for this book, has allowed me to continue to move forward in God's grace and still flourish amidst so many bad choices.

The harsh reality is many of my dreams just won't come

true—they can no longer come true. And I'm left to come to grips that, since the day I left college, my life has gone differently than I ever thought it would.

Life rarely turns out as we planned, and reality always wins. Sometimes it's because of other people's choices. Most of the time, though, it's because of our own choices that are now generously paying back consequences with overwhelming interest:

- Your marriage might not be happily ever after.
- You never need to purchase a highchair.
- You might not get to walk your daughter down the aisle.
- The second marriage feels a lot like the first marriage.
- The prodigal son may not be coming home.
- Your career will never be what you want, and you feel stuck.
- Your health inhibits your life, and you simply don't have answers.

And if any of the above (or others that have come to mind) make you want to skip this chapter, I urge you to just hold on and keep reading. I've been and still am you. But four little words we'll discuss may provide just the hope you need moving forward.

If you're at a place in your life where your dreams aren't or can't come true, oftentimes anger and panic set in. And the first one to get blamed is God. He promised you. You feel God owes you because of *your* obedience. Or maybe you feel like God granted someone else *your* wish.

What do we do when our dreams can't come true? Let's explore what David did in his situation.

Twenty-two years after becoming king and in his 50s, King David's story took a turn that set him on a course that would have tremendous consequences for himself and his family. It began with Bathsheba and the extremes David went to in order to cover his tracks. But as author Andy Stanley observes, "Every sin comes prepackaged with a consequence."

Nathan the Prophet's words would be spoken: "God will bring calamity on you and your family."

TEN LONG YEARS LATER THE CONSEQUENCE HAPPENS:

1. **Rape of Tamar** (there are no secrets in the palace): David was furious but did nothing. And who was he to say anything?

2. **Absalom:** Murdered his brother Amnon for his blatant sin against his own family, then came back to overthrow the kingdom (it's mine anyway, I'm going to take it early.) He stole the hearts of the people over four years.

3. **Nathan the Prophet:** Remember that temple you wanted to build? About that...

Two scenarios jolt David's reality that his legacy is going to look completely different than his early days of nothing-but-success.

Scenario #1: Sixteen years after the Bathsheba incident, his consequences come full circle. King David was now a sixty-one year old fugitive. This was not the dream.

Scenario #2: Nathan the Prophet took back his original reaction to David wanting to build the first permanent temple of God.

We discussed the first scenario when we looked at David as a Family Man, and we touched on the second scenario as David as a Leader. But what we didn't drill down on was the loss of his dreams, ones that just could not and would not come true.

This is the hard reality of life, and people handle it in different ways:

1. A life of disappointment and just settling for the hand that they've been dealt
2. Pursuing happiness any way they can that all too often is only about the here-and-now
3. Passive-aggressiveness like a low-grade fever taking their crushed dreams out on everyone around them

Some people, however, come to grips with their harsh reality and allow God to come in. These rare people allow Him to not only heal this pain but do something *with* it. Easy to tell someone else to do, seemingly impossible when it's you needing to hear these words.

Now, this is where our story intersects with King David. Maybe you are feeling like God could've intervened in your story but didn't, and you're feeling the weight of His absence. And if you're anything like me, this is usually when we make things worse and create more personal pain. We adopt the "whatever man" attitude and puts a "whatever-like existence" into our life because we leave God completely out of it. "He had His chance to make this right," but because our lives didn't turn out like the original script, "He's out and I'm back in charge."

Been there? I don't just own the t-shirt, I'm the one who was printing them in mass quantities. I'm *that* guy.

The irony in David's story is the biographer never withholds David's sin. But David, amidst all his mistakes, never lost his confidence in God. Whether someone else's or his own fault, he stayed true in his faith in God. Did he have seasons of silence and times of seeming to avoid God? Absolutely. But he never remained there. He came to these realities:

Every time I do my will, I miss things up.

Every time I have my way, I get in the way.

Not my will, but Thy will.

The foundation of our faith is not answered prayer, everything going our way, and happily-ever-after endings.

"It's always a mistake to measure our faith in God or our confidence in God in our dreams coming true."[117]

"If my dreams come true, God is good.

If my dreams don't come true, I don't believe there's a God.

It's always a mistake to wrap our dreams or even our answers to pray around our circumstances. Dreams that don't come true or prayers that don't get answered say nothing of God's presence or lack of activity. Let me say that last sentence one more time because it's easy to miss but vitally critical to your trust in God: Dreams that don't come true or prayers that don't get answered say nothing of God's presence or lack of activity.

David would be the quickest to remind us: We're mistaken when we feel forsaken."[118] God's lack of felt presence does not mean He's absent. It's like a father at a safe distance with his kids to see what they're doing, how they're handling a situation but just close enough to show up when he feels the timing is right.

I've learned through years of experience that "Through all the highs and lows, God is always with me." And often the lows are very low. This is when God teaches me that He never offered me "rescue faith" there to swoop in like a rescue parent at the first chance of a problem. He loves me too much and wants me to learn, grow, and trust that He's there, especially during the times when my dreams and plans can no longer come true.

The hardest lesson to learn when your life is not turning out as planned is, I may lose my world but not lose my confidence or my faith in God. Catch the depth in that last statement:

I may lose my world but not lose my confidence or my faith in God.

This is the difference between just existing and a flourishing life. And this is where four small and powerful words apply:

Even though...I will...

In the reading at the top of this chapter, Habakkuk the prophet said, *even though* there's no harvest, and *even though* crops fail, and *even though* fields are desolate, and *even though* the stalls of provision are empty, *I will* still be joyful and glad because the Lord God is my Savior.

I have not lost my faith. In fact, my faith is even greater. I'm still going to worship God. When I encounter hard times and broken dreams, my faith inflates.

"This is not the faith of a Christian [a road warrior after God's own heart] who believes in God only when the sun shines. This is not a faith that wilts under pressure or life-altering disappointments. This faith flourishes even though my plans can't come true.

This faith says, 'Even though bad things are happening, I will praise the Lord.'

Question: how might you personalize Habakkuk's prayer in your own situation with your own altered dreams and change of plans?

Even though…I will…

Even though…I will…

Even though…I will…

Developing this kind of 'even though / I will' faith changes the temperature and trajectory of your life. When the pressure mounts, this kind of faith doesn't deflate. Instead, it actually inflates. It becomes bolder. More resolute and undaunted. The development of an 'even though' kind of faith has a lot to do with where we position our focus."[119]

I'm not saying there is not pain and loss in your dreams and plans that can't come true. You may still have more mourning to do or learn to mourn on a consistent basis when you're confronted with this reality.

My counselor is teaching me that right now in my life with my two oldest boys from a previous marriage. He's teaching it to me regarding the original direction of my life being hijacked and imploding, thanks to my own selfish actions that still haunt me to this day.

But I'm also learning the power of Habakkuk's prayer: Even though…I will…

David, after all the professional victories and personal defeats, demonstrated this humble posture towards God.

Every time I do my will, I miss things up.

Every time I have my way, I get in the way.

Not my will, but Thy will.

QUESTION

What dreams or plans can't come true in your life, and how are you handling that reality right now?

TODAY'S ROAD PRAYER

God, coming to terms with my life's disappointments is difficult beyond words. I'll be honest, I don't want to come to terms with broken dreams and change of plans. I want my life to be going the way I had planned.

But the reality is different, and I am here right now with a choice to blame, resent, self-medicate, and give-up on life. Or I can acknowledge that You're still with me and have lessons that You can teach me. You can still grow my faith in ways that the easy times will never develop in me.

I want an *Even Though...I Will* faith that changes my future. May You soften my heart to this posture, allowing You to do what needs to be done in my heart right now.

I give you THIS DAY to become a road warrior after Your own heart.

Write down your own version of *Even though... I will...* statements and review them throughout the rest of this road trip.

6.4 SUCCESSION

Handing Off the Legacy

And David said, "My son Solomon is young and inexperienced, and the house that is to be built for the LORD shall be exceedingly magnificent, famous and glorious throughout all lands. Therefore now I will make preparation for it." So David made ample preparations before his death. What a father! He may have been weak at other times, but at this moment, David stands tall. "Lord, I know You don't want me to fulfill the dream, but, Lord, I'm going to set apart as much as I can to support my son as he fulfills the dream that was on my heart" (1 Chronicles 22:5-6 ESV).

If you seek Him, He will be found by You; but if You forsake Him, He will cast you off forever.

David also said to Solomon his son, "Be strong and courageous, and do the work. Do not be afraid or discouraged, for the Lord God, my God, is with you. He will not fail you or forsake you until all the work for the service of the temple of the Lord is finished" (1 Chronicles 28:9b,20 NCB).

Handing off your legacy means different things to different people. It may mean handing off the family business or hoping your family caught what you were trying to model throughout your years. Too many, sadly, leave their legacy to chance.

Personally, I don't want to be remembered for my implosion in the first half of my life, but for overcoming and allowing God to redeem my story through my surrender to Him the rest of my life.

DAVID PASSED ON TWO MAJOR PARTS OF HIS LEGACY:

1. His Faults

I can't help but wonder if David the King ever spoke to Solomon as David the Father about his mistakes in life and what he hoped his son would avoid. After all, Solomon's mother was part of one of the most infamous stories of adultery of all time. If David had this difficult but needed father-son conversation, Solomon definitely was zoning out. He would have many of his father's struggles, especially with women. He had over 700 wives and countless concubines. Talk about the original "one-up" kinda guy.

We also know there were other children of David beyond the most noted ones in Scripture. We don't know how they responded to David's faults and if they learned from them or if they repeated the sins of the father.

That's the scary part of the example we set. There are two crucial elements: what we say and what we do. Both are critical. Unfortunately, we only see the latter in the life of David. He was apparently so overwhelmed by his past faults that he never used them as teaching moments with his children. Huge, missed opportunities. And even though each person makes their own choices, we can set up children up for a harder row by not talking with them, now and often.

I've made some huge mistakes that have had severe consequences. I have been so convicted by this part of David's life that I need to swallow my pride, embrace the awkward conversation, and serve my children by these needed conversations from their one and only father. I hope you're feeling the same conviction and are willing to do the same.

Sadly, this is where too many of us stop the story: in our past. Like us, David was more than just his faults and mistakes. He had something of true value he could pass on as a legacy.

2. His Faith

David, despite all his faults, did have a faith like none other his entire life. Solomon started strong but was swayed and distracted later in his life by the gods of the many wives he took. Not David. Faults, yes, but he always submitted to God's laws and was hence a man after God's own heart.

"How is it that David at the end of his days, in passing the baton to his son Solomon, could say, 'Be strong and courageous, and do the work. Do not be afraid or discouraged, for the Lord God, my God, is with you. He will not fail you or forsake you until all the work for the service of the temple of the Lord is finished.' It is precisely because this was the whole story of David's life. God had been faithful to David. Through all the dilemmas of his life—the times of rebellion, rejection, and repentance—the elder statesman of Israel knew one thing! God had stayed with him."[120]

Maybe this was David's way of saying (at least to Solomon) that no matter all the mistakes we make, God will be with you. The good times and victories, and the tough times and losses. I can only imagine the passion and emotion in sharing these words. Maybe David's boldness came back at the end of his life to make sure at least one of his children knew that his faith was what made him truly different. It was the one constant throughout his life.

David was handing off what God allowed him to build in the kingdom of Israel, and now Solomon was given the kingdom and the opportunity to build the temple. This is where David was able to influence his son with all the planning he had done, setting his son up for his legacy.

I truly believe our legacy is two-part: faults and faith. Our children must see congruence between how we handle our faith even in the midst of our failures. The easy way out is to simply act like they never existed, if it's possible to hide them. Most of the time that is the case, but it doesn't ultimately serve our family. They desperately need to see God at work *through* our failures, the lessons God has taught and continues to teach us, and how they can learn from our own faults.

As for faults, I have many, and we're navigating when to share the most potent ones with some of my children. I also need to revisit those conversations with my older sons while they're still under my roof because those days are numbered.

One conversation we've had is why Dad chose to stop drinking for good. My kids thankfully never saw the ugly side of my drinking. But they have seen the variety, inconsistency, and dependency that was magnified by life on the road. I'm admitting why and often to them, which is embarrassing and humbling. Yet God is using my weakness to show them growth and victory in this area of my life that had a stronghold for decades.

Other conversations, such as my addiction to porn for a season on the road, is yet another delicate conversation where my faith must supersede my faults.

> *You have faults and faith that are part of your current legacy, road warrior. The question is, are you allowing God to redeem your story, with all the faults, to grow your faith?*

My fear is that I've waited too long to share my journey with my kids. Missed opportunities for teachable moments because I didn't want the awkwardness, the questions, the embarrassment. But this is so selfish and unloving.

Handing off the legacy doesn't have to be "one major moment." It can be teachable moments all along the way. This is the point of this chapter. But how do you take the next step?

1. **Take an inventory of your faults**: What are the past failures and struggles you've worked through or are currently working through in your life right now?

2. **Assess the progress**: Where are you with those past failures and struggles? Are there any areas that need more growth?

3. **Uncover the lessons learned:** What has God taught or been teaching you in these areas? Write them down and find the gold you can pass on.

4. **Embrace the awkwardness**: Going in, know that this will be difficult to bring up, but it is worth it in the long run.

5. **Make the time**: Since these conversations may be awkward, they won't "just come up." Make the time that will allow these conversations to be uninterrupted and received.

6. **Pray, Pray, Pray**: Ask God to give you wisdom and courage that He will guide you during these times.

7. **Prepare for their response**: There may be questions, but there also may be complete silence. Both are okay.

Some of these steps may require a difficult conversation with a friend, pastor, or professional counselor. I'll admit that I needed all three!

The older I get, the more I care about my legacy to my wife and children. I'm especially more aware of how my failures in the past have and will affect their future. But I've also had enough of letting the past paralyze me that I'm willing to embrace the awkward conversation and allow my family to enter my journey.

This all leads back to becoming a road warrior after God's own heart: one who cares about the things of God and who leverages the gift of David's life to reveal areas in our own lives that need attention.

QUESTION

At this point in your life, how would you be remembered to your significant other and/or children?

TODAY'S ROAD PRAYER

God, I am challenged and convicted in handing off my legacy to others. It's an area I've not put much thought into until now. And it's an area that is easy to put off, yet needs to be addressed.

As painful as they may be, bring my faults to the surface so I can evaluate what has healed and what still needs healing. Guide me on the lessons You've taught me in these areas.

I give you THIS DAY to become a road warrior after Your own heart.

Write down how your faith needs to grow amidst your faults. This is one that may take some time, but working through the faults vs. faith is so critical to becoming a road warrior after God's own heart.

6.5 LESSONS

What We Need to Learn from David's Life

But the Lord said to Samuel, "Do not consider his appearance or his height, for I have rejected him. The Lord does not look at the things people look at. People look at the outward appearance, but the Lord looks at the heart."

Then the Lord said, "Rise and anoint him; this is the one." So Samuel took the horn of oil and anointed him in the presence of his brothers, and from that day on the Spirit of the Lord came powerfully upon David (1 Samuel 16:7, 12b, 13 NET).

What a story. What a life. You just can't make this stuff up. And mad kudos to the Bible for not hiding the raw, unfiltered side of this iconic man's life.

But what have we really learned from this man now that we've come to the end?

SEVEN IMPORTANT LESSONS FROM THE LIFE OF DAVID

Lesson One: David had serious emotional family wounds to overcome.

We learned this very early in the story of his life with being virtually invisible to his father and verbally abused by his brothers. This was not a great way to build security and confidence in the formative years of life, but it was the hand that was dealt to David.

These emotional wounds would manifest themselves throughout David's life. He was hurt over and over by many which would surface time and time again.

The key was in how David handled these painful moments in his life. Often, he turned to God to receive healing, especially when the wound with Saul was never healed. In another situation, grace healed the wounds, with his family meeting him in his lonely days in the desert.

What About You? The reality is that we all deal with emotional wounds we need to overcome. They can either taint every major season of our lives or become areas of growth and victory when we allow God to heal these painful places in our lives.

Lesson Two: David's strengths were also his weaknesses.

David had so many strengths that it almost seems unfair how blessed he was in this area. This can cause jealousy and resentment when we compare ourselves to others.

He was known for his passion, and it made him great—from his music and poetry to his faith in God and leadership.

His ability to lead people, though, also gave him the ability to manipulate and control people.

His passion for people led to accumulating wives and concubines that didn't even satisfy his sexual desire. We see this clearly in the episode with Bathsheba, which in turn led to a lifetime of painful consequences.

What About You? We need to look at our strengths and see the areas where, though God meant them for good, we could easily allow the evil one to use them for bad. Others who know and care for us are often the very ones who can offer this very difficult but valuable intel about ourselves.

Lesson Three: David was either all in or all out.
Did you notice that every part of David's life was one extreme or the other?

- Fighting bears to fighting soldiers
- Leading armies to leading refugees
- Adultery to cover-ups
- Creating children to not disciplining them

There is a quote in my book, *Elite Road Warrior: Six Energy Habits to Master the Business Travel Life,* (and a theme throughout it) that is applicable to this specific lesson:

> *"If you want to do something, you'll find a way. If you don't, you'll find excuse." –Jim Rohn*

That was David. When he wanted to do something, he was all in and found a way, even over insurmountable odds. But when he didn't want to do something, he was all out and found an excuse.

What About You? Do you find this to be true of you on the road? Either you're in a good place spiritually—you're reading your Bible, praying, and feel close to God. Or you're out of the spiritual rhythm and it's hit-and-miss at best. My prayer is this book has been a catalyst for you being "all in" and hopefully gaining some powerful momentum as a road warrior after God's own heart.

Lesson Four: When David was angry, alone, or afraid, he defaulted to taking matters into his own hands.
This is a natural default of most men, and it's especially true of those business travelers who hold a position of power.

Author Andy Stanley reminds us, "The ways of God are most

unappealing and they seem the most irrelevant when we're angry, alone, or afraid."

If we're in the "all out" of lesson three and not in a good place with God, this may describe how we're feeling when we feel out of control. And if we're living with some secret sins on the road, we're doing everything we can to keep the cover-up going. I know and I get it because I've been there.

When I drank on the road, I was the 2-for-1 guy at happy hour, then wine for dinner, then a top shelf bourbon as a nightcap. And this was only day one of a four-day trip! Tomorrow would be a new city with new people. It gave me a false sense of control and a downward spiral.

When I was struggling with porn for a period of time on the road, this was exactly my means of operation until I was caught. I was in a dark and isolated place that needed to be exposed and corrected.

What About You? If you were to be brutally honest with me right now as I just chose to be with you, are you seeking to control circumstances in your life all the while feeling angry, alone, or afraid?

My prayer is that if you're in a similar place of (insert road sin here) that you'll relinquish control back to God and find healing. Now.

Lesson Five: David misinterpreted his success and popularity as a sign of God's blanket approval on all he was doing.
This is a scary place to be, and I've been there. It's called *entitlement*.

For example, David's journey lead him to reside in the land of the Philistines (remember, some giant dude he stoned was from that land.) Our main character was living directly out of God's will in many ways, yet he still prospered. This is what makes it so easy to misinterpret and misconstrue these events as God's blessing on David's life.

But we do the same thing on the road. We may be hiding some pretty heavy sin, yet we're killing it on the road right now. Popularity and income are high, despite the sinful behavior you are allowing to continue.

What About You? Are you feeling a sense of entitlement and justifying your behavior just because work is going well?

Learn from David's lesson here that success at work does not excuse any disobedience to God. If we're not careful, our spiritual life in the eyes of God can be deteriorating while our "greatness" in the eyes of men can be increasing. This was tragic for David and could eventually be true of us. This mindset, this *justification*, could lead to a self-inflicted implosion—a Bathsheba, a broken family, and children who turn against you and God.

Lesson Six: David's great sins of adultery and murder disqualified him from correcting and disciplining his own children for the same sins.

What could David seriously say to his son Amnon when he had raped his own sister, Tamar? What right did David have to deal with his son Absalom when he, in turn, murdered Amnon for raping his sister?

Obviously, he still had the responsibility to discipline his own children even though he had committed sins just as flagrant and offensive. But how could he say absolutely anything in good conscience? No doubt David played through exactly how this scene would go, bringing up these transgressions to any one of his kids:

"What right do you have to deal with me for my behavior when *you*, the king, a man after God's own heart, have committed a similar crime?"

This may be the origin of the phrase: "Do as I say and not as I do."

David never seemed to overcome this problem. His loss of respect was just too great. Forgiven? Absolutely. Justified and exonerated in the eyes of his people and of his own children? Not a chance. He bore this cross of his failures to his death.

What About You? Do you feel that, because of your past, you've lost the right to parent the way you've been called to do? Or if you don't have kids, how about your integrity in leading people?

Fortunately, most of us have not come anywhere close to blowing it to the level of iconic David. And in most instances, children are very understanding and forgiving *if* and *when* they see true repentance and ownership of our part.

And this is the lesson for us: that we become vulnerable to our children in age-appropriate ways so that we don't forfeit our ability to discipline our own children. This is a hard lesson to learn, but my prayer is that it's one you can and want to learn.

Lesson Seven: Each time David owned and repented of his sin, God forgave him and restored their relationship.

Though David on several occasions walked out of God's will with his eyes wide open, there came a point in his life—a defining moment, many times—where he turned back to God with great remorse and sorrow to seek God's forgiveness. In many respects, this is why he was called a man after God's own heart.

How can we prove it? Just read the Psalms. Chapters 32 and 51 are so graphic of the physical and emotional consequences of David's sin and its effect, not only on his own life but how he hurt the heart of God.

And this is where David is different and such a great example for us on the road.

- David excelled in an aspect of his life then took matters into his own hands.
- Like the prodigal son, David "came to his senses" and came back to God.
- David owns his behavior and truly repents of his sin.
- God graciously and consistently forgives David and restores their relationship.

Wash. Rinse. Repeat.

What About You? Do you find yourself right now as one who blows it before God then hides? Or could you be more like David by learning this lesson of owning and repenting of your sin before a holy God and being restored? Or before the consequences even happen?

My prayer for all of us on the road is this: regardless of our poor choices that separate us from God, we may always, *always*, come back to God with a humble heart of contrition. May we seek restoration with a God who forgives us and loves us like none other.

QUESTION

Which of these seven lessons resonates the most with you in this very moment?

TODAY'S ROAD PRAYER

God, there are so many lessons from the life of David that apply to me. But I know you have one specific lesson you want me to learn and apply right now.

May I listen to that "still small voice" as You reveal to me what You would have me learn and how I should grow.

Speak, Lord, for Your servant is listening.

I give you THIS DAY—and every day after this one—to become a road warrior after Your own heart.

Write down the specific lesson you feel God has prompted for you to learn from the life of David. How do you plan to apply it to your life on the road moving forward?

CONCLUSION

HOW TO BE A ROAD WARRIOR AFTER GOD'S OWN HEART

The question I wrestled with in David's life is, *"How could a man who deceived, committed adultery, murder, cover-up his sin, had multiple wives and concubines, and was a passive, absent, and inconsistent father still be a man after God's own heart?"*

This is an amazing and unfiltered story of one man's life, and it's one we can truly relate to on the road.

- We experienced David as a no-name.
- We experienced David as a warrior.
- We experienced David as a loner.
- We experienced David as a leader.
- We experienced David as a family man.
- We experienced David as a legacy.

It's so easy to forget his no-name season that developed his outer and inner skills. We over-emphasize and even glorify his season as a warrior from his Goliath-size victory and amazing confidence in God to his incredible fame. We resonate with his leadership while we easily gloss over his legacy. In fact, this entire book was about his legacy!

But in the end, I specifically noticed what David did not do: lead his family. As I studied David as a Fam Man, my heart broke for David as a father. For him to have such success in his work yet be so anemic in his own little kingdom of his family is scary. And it's so easy to allow this to happen. His legacy as a father left generations of scars and carnage.

And how about the intense therapy all his kids would've needed as a result of this dark season of David's life. Sometimes no amount of counseling brings someone back from parental-inflicted wounds.

I hear it often from road warrior men who somehow see me as their priest as they confess their shortcomings as a husband and father. Why me, when they've rarely if ever told another soul? Maybe because I asked tough questions and gave them room and permission to become real.

I am successful on the road. I feel the "praises of men" on a consistent basis. All too often, though, I can be important on the road but invisible at home. I can be killing it on the road but getting killed at home. I can lead on the road and be lazy at home. I'm passionate on the road but, sadly, pathetic at home.

And who is affected by my bipolar attitude and actions? My family.

I want, I need, and I long to be a road warrior after God's own heart. But it doesn't start when I get home. It starts on the road. Right now. Right here. And it must continue on the road no matter the city, the length of trip, or the challenges of the road.

This book came to be out of a desire to learn valuable lessons from the life of David. What I didn't expect was just how extreme the lessons were that I would learn from his life. High highs and very low lows. I also didn't realize just how much I saw myself in David's life when looking through the eyes of a business traveler. This perspective changed everything for me, and this book had to be written. For you, and for me.

My hope is that you will live a different life as the result of immersing your own life vicariously through David.

My prayer is that you have a newfound desire to be a road warrior after God's own heart.

But the decision is yours. Only you can have this heart that is often in direct contrast to your life on the road. It's not popular. It's not desired. It's not celebrated. It's not easy. It's not sought after by most around you.

In fact, if anything they'll do their best to thwart your best laid plans that you made that very morning. The irony is they don't realize they're even doing it, but we're not of this world.

Our position as those who've chosen to bear the name of Jesus Christ is to daily take up our cross and follow Him.

His will.

His way.

His timing.

No matter the challenges of the road.

This unique road warrior spiritual life is worth pursuing and fighting. It does lead to becoming a road warrior after God's own heart.

MY CLOSING PRAYER FOR YOU

God, may You alone continue to develop this desire You've placed in the holder of this book—a desire to daily seek You and honor You on the road, no matter what season as a business traveler they find themselves in.

Guard their heart.

Renew their mind.

Guide their steps.

Awaken their soul.

May You reward their investment in learning from the life of David, that they will live their life on the road different from this day forward.

Encourage them when times are tough.

Forgive them when they confess their sin.

Lead them when the path is unclear.

Strengthen them when their flesh is weak.

God, come along side this business traveler as they seek to become a road warrior after Your own heart.

With full confidence, I pray that Your will be done in their life on the road.

Amen.

With the utmost respect,
A fellow road warrior after God's own heart

ABOUT THE AUTHOR

Bryan Paul Buckley is a business travel performance expert who is an experienced road warrior, traveling both domestically and internationally. He's traveled as the bottom of the barrel manager to the height of a vice president and knows the challenges of both worlds. He's pushed so hard on the road that he was sidelined with major health issues that could've been avoided. He also found himself 40 pounds overweight and struggled with energy until one day "had enough," making major life changes that produced tremendous results in every area of his road life.

He's the husband of one and father of five and lives with his family in the Chicagoland area. He understands the importance of family and the challenge of staying connected on the road.

Bryan Paul Buckley is an author, speaker, and corporate trainer who wants to help exhausted and existing road warriors to become elite road warriors who master the business travel life.

But most importantly, Bryan Paul Buckley is a devout Christian who struggles and strives to live out his faith every day on the road. He writes with experience and understands the challenges of a Christian business traveler who seeks to become a road warrior after God's own heart.

ADDITIONAL RESOURCES

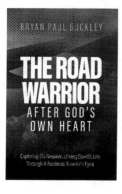

Elite Road Warrior:
Six Energy Habits to Master
the Business Travel Life

The Elite Road Warrior is written for the business traveler by a business traveler who understands the real challenges to becoming elite in the areas that matter most: your work, health, and home life.

In this book, you will learn:

- How to Increase Results Without Working Non-Stop
- How to Get Fit on the Road Without A Lot of Time
- How to Actually Eat Healthy on the Road Without Coming Close to Starving
- How to Rest to be at Your Best on the Road Without Sacrificing Productivity
- How to Invest in Yourself in Personal and Professional Areas
- How to Stay Connected With Those Back Home Without Reacting All the Time

Elite Business Travel Boss:
The Unwritten Success Guide for Leading Business Travel Teams

It's one thing to be the boss of a team, it's an entirely different thing to be the boss of a business travel team. It's hard enough to manage a team that is right in front of you, or even remote people who are always in one place. But how do you manage a team that is literally all over the place in different cities and time zones?

Therein lies the challenge that few business travel bosses have yet to figure out.

Elite Business Travel Boss is the unwritten success guide to leading business travel teams. It will help you become not just good, but an elite business travel boss—one that every business traveler wants to work for and never wants to leave. One who eliminates burnout and exceeds results under your leadership.

In This Book, You Will Learn

- The six misbeliefs business travel team leaders believe
- The six objections you need to consider
- The five questions you want answered
- The six return-on-investments you can implement using the Elite Road Warrior Method
- Three actions expected of you as the business travel team leader
- Three responsibilities you absolutely must do to succeed as the business travel team leader

The *Elite Road Warrior Podcast*
Insert Elite Road Warrior Podcast image

If you travel for business, you live in a whole other world that most simply don't understand. They think it's an easy and glamorous life. But the road can be hard. It can be difficult to be both productive and effective. It's a challenge to stay healthy and it's a battle to stay connected with those you love back home. Too many business travelers are on auto-pilot and just plain burned out. But it doesn't have to be this way.

You want to be at your best no matter where you are, especially on the road, but rarely are we taught how to master the business travel life. Until now. *The Elite Road Warrior* Podcast is for the business traveler who wants to transform their work, health, and home life while on the road.

Professionally recorded from a road warrior to a road warrior, *The Elite Road Warrior* Podcast is structured with odd-numbered episodes focusing on topics relating to the Six Energy Habits. Even-numbered episodes feature interviews with subject matter experts. Each episode is only 30-40 minutes to maximize your time on the road.

Corporate Keynotes and Workshops

Have you ever considered training your business travelers by an actual professional business traveler? Bryan Paul Buckley, the founder of Elite Road Warrior, offers specific training on the three focus areas of an elite road warrior:

- Work
- Health
- Home Life

When one or more of these focus areas are off in any way, performance is affected. But when all three are dialed in and running smoothly, you have just created an elite road warrior.

Elite Road Warrior offers everything from a one-hour keynote and half-day seminars to full-day workshops and consulting.

If interested in bringing Bryan Paul Buckley for your audience or event, please inquire here: **www.eliteroadwarrior.com**

Christian Business Traveler Speaker

Almost every single church has a business traveler in their congregation and too many churches are simply unaware of the challenges they face on any given business trip. They need someone who understands their world as a road warrior from their work to their health, to their home life but also their spiritual life.

What if the church became a true resource for this unique and needed group in the business world?

Most churches understandably wouldn't know where to begin.

Until now.

I encourage you to allow me to come in to speak to your business travelers in a way that will not only help them at the event but also create a community of spiritual road warriors locally and nationally.

You can do something, and I can help.

If you're a spiritual road warrior and feel your church could benefit from this option, make the introduction.

Please reach out to us to begin this conversation: Bryan@ BryanPaulBuckley.com

ACKNOWLEDGMENTS

Oddly enough, thank you King David for living a life that can serve as a raw, unfiltered example, especially for a business traveler who desires to be a road warrior after God's own heart. You left us so many lessons in each of the six seasons of your life that we have a blueprint on how to live on the road.

Dr. Nick Howard for his ongoing counsel that has worked me through my own messes on the road and encouraged me to be a road warrior after God's own heart I've longed to become.

The Buck Fam: my wife, Susan and the kiddos—Trey, Kole, Kaitlyn, Kaleb, and Austin. You've been patient with my business travel through the years. You've shown me grace and loved me through the thick and thicker days. You inspire me to become the husband and father you deserve, and the one God has called me to become for you.

The still, soft voice of the Holy Spirit who has prompted, guided, corrected, and consoled me on the road.

ENDNOTES AND SOURCES

INTRODUCTION

1   McKenzie, Steven L.. King David: A Biography (United Kingdom: Oxford University Press, 2000)

2   Rutland, Mark . "David the Great: Why King David's Name and Fame Have Endured through the Ages." *Ministry Today* (Lake Mary, FL), March/April 2018, 14.

3   Rutland, Mark. "David The Great: Why King David's Name and Fame Have Endured through the Ages."

4   Rutland, Mark. David The Great: Deconstructing the Man After God's Own Heart. United States (Charisma House, 2018), 4.

5   Mast, Dale L.. And David Perceived He Was King (United States: XULON Press, 2015), 93-94.

6   Park, J.. The Life of King David: How God Works Through Ordinary Outcasts and Extraordinary Sinners (Independently published, 2015), 1.

1.1 RUNT

7   Lucado, Max. Facing Your Giants: God Still Does the Impossible (United States: Thomas Nelson, 2020), 15.

8   Park, J.. The Life of King David: How God Works Through Ordinary Outcasts and Extraordinary Sinners, 16.

1.3 INTERNAL

9   Redpath, Alan. The Making of a Man of God: Lessons from the Life of David (United States: Baker Publishing Group, 2004), 17-18.

10 "What Is Solitude?" *Psychology Today*, Sussex Publishers, https://www.psychologytoday.com/us/articles/200307/what-is-solitude.

11 Swindoll, Charles R.. David: A Man of Passion & Destiny: Profiles in Character (United States: Word Publishing, 1997), 10.

12 https://www.merriam-webster.com/dictionary/trust

13 Jung, Joanne, and Rick Langer. "The Strange Tale of How Nicholas Herman Found Meaning in Life." The Good Book Blog. October 31, 2022. https://www.biola.edu/blogs/good-book-blog/2022/the-strange-tale-of-how-nicholas-herman-found-meaning-in-life.

1.4 OVERLOOKED

14 Webb, Jonice PhD. "Feel Overlooked Sometimes? This May Be The Reason." PsychCentral. March 26, 2017. https://psychcentral.com/blog/childhood-neglect/2017/03/feel-overlooked-sometimes-this-may-be-the-reason#1.

15 Park, J.. The Life of King David: How God Works Through Ordinary Outcasts and Extraordinary Sinners, 20.

16 Swindoll, Charles R.. David: A Man of Passion and Destiny, 17-18.

17 Lucado, Max. Facing Your Giants: God Still Does the Impossible, 15.

18 Batterson, Mark. Win the Day: 7 Daily Habits to Help You Stress Less & Accomplish More (United States: Crown Publishing Group, 2020), 33.

19 Swindoll, Charles R.. David: A Man of Passion and Destiny, 20.

20 Mast, Dale L.. And David Perceived He Was King, 55.

21 Wolpe, David. David: The Divided Heart. United States: Yale University Press, 2014. p. 2.

22 Lucado, Max. Facing Your Giants: God Still Does the Impossible, 16.

1.5 REVEAL

23 Park, J.. The Life of King David: How God Works Through Ordinary Outcasts and Extraordinary Sinners, 21.

24 Rutland, Mark. David The Great: Deconstructing the Man After God's Own Heart. p. 14.

25 Redpath, Alan. The Making of a Man of God: Lessons from the Life of David.

2.1 MANAGEMENT

26 Young Entreprenuers Council. "12 Traits Bad Bosses Have In Common." Forbes. September 25, 2018. https://www.forbes.com/sites/theyec/2018/09/25/12-traits-bad-bosses-have-in-common/?sh=517b24256266.

27 Swindoll, Charles R.. David: A Man of Passion and Destiny, 30.

28 Mast, Dale L.. And David Perceived He Was King, 64.

2.2 STONED

29 Swindoll, Charles R.. David: A Man of Passion and Destiny, 38.

30 Rutland, Mark. David The Great: Deconstructing the Man After God's Own Heart, 30.

31 Gladwell, Malcolm. David and Goliath: Underdogs, Misfits, and the Art of Battling Giants (United States: Little, Brown, 2013), 11.

32 Lucado, Max. Facing Your Giants: God Still Does the Impossible, 5.

33 Rutland, Mark. David The Great: Deconstructing the Man After God's Own Heart, 34.

2.3 POPULARITY

34 Swindoll, Charles R.. David: A Man of Passion and Destiny, 51.

35 Swindoll, Charles R.. David: A Man of Passion and Destiny, 55.

36 Rutland, Mark. David The Great: Deconstructing the Man After God's Own Heart, 40.

37 Mast, Dale L.. And David Perceived He Was King, 118.

2.4 DISCERNMENT

38 "Five Smooth Stones." Bible.Org. February 2, 2009. https://bible.org/illustration/five-smooth-stones.

39 Rutland, Mark. David The Great: Deconstructing the Man After God's Own Heart, 31.

40 Swindoll, Charles R.. David: A Man of Passion and Destiny, 44.

41 Swindoll, Charles R.. David: A Man of Passion and Destiny, 47.

2.5 LOYALTY

42 Rutland, Mark. David The Great: Deconstructing the Man After God's Own Heart, 45.

43 "The Three Gifts." Going Beyond the Familiar. December 9, 2013. http://www.goingbeyondthefamiliar.com/2013/12/three-gifts.html.

44 "The Three Gifts." Going Beyond the Familiar.

3.1 CRUTCHES

45 Adapted from Swindoll, Charles R.. David: A Man of Passion and Destiny, 62-66.

46 Nelson, Alan E.. Broken in the Right Place (United States: T. Nelson Publishers, 1994.)

3.2 DECEPTION

47 Stanley, Andy. "David." (Series). Your Move with Andy Stanley. May 15, 2018. Video, https://www.youtube.com/watch?v=wW1AoyzUpHU&t=7s.

3.3 DESPERATION

48   Peterson, Eugene H.. First and Second Samuel (United Kingdom: Presbyterian Publishing Corporation, 1999), 112.

49   Swindoll, Charles R.. David: A Man of Passion and Destiny, 72-73.

50   Arnold, Bill T.. 1 and 2 Samuel (United States: Zondervan, 2014), 311.

3.4 DISRESPECTED

51   Stanley, Andy. "David." (Series).

52   Getz, Gene A.. When You Feel Like a Failure (United States: Gospel Light Publications, 1984), 112.

3.5 TIMING

53   Kirsch, Jonathan. King David: The Real Life of the Man Who Ruled Israel. United Kingdom: Random House Publishing Group, 2009. p. 105.

54   Stanley, Andy. "David." (Series).

55   Stanley, Andy. "David." (Series).

4.1 CHOICE

56   Arnold, Bill T.. 1 and 2 Samuel, 418.

57   Stanley, Andy. "David." (Series).

4.2 NEVERTHELESS

58   Rutland, Mark. David The Great: Deconstructing the Man After God's Own Heart, 90.

59   Lucado, Max. Facing Your Giants: God Still Does the Impossible, 97.

60   Kirsch, Jonathan. King David: The Real Life of the Man Who Ruled Israel, 151.

61   Arnold, Bill T.. 1 and 2 Samuel, 454.

62   Lucado, Max. Facing Your Giants: God Still Does the Impossible, 97.

63   Lucado, Max. Facing Your Giants: God Still Does the Impossible, 99.

64   Lucado, Max. Facing Your Giants: God Still Does the Impossible, 99.

65   Lucado, Max. Facing Your Giants: God Still Does the Impossible, 100.

66   Lucado, Max. Facing Your Giants: God Still Does the Impossible, 101.

4.3 COMPASSION

67   Peterson, Eugene H.. First and Second Samuel, 172.

68   Lucado, Max. Facing Your Giants: God Still Does the Impossible, 112-113.

69   Peterson, Eugene H.. First and Second Samuel, 174.

70 Brueggemann, Walter. First and Second Samuel: Interpretation: A Bible Commentary for Teaching and Preaching (United States: Presbyterian Publishing Corporation, 2012), 267.

71 Lucado, Max. Facing Your Giants: A David and Goliath Story for Everyday People (United States: W Publishing Group, 2006), 115-116.

72 Swindoll, Charles R.. David: A Man of Passion and Destiny, 176-178.

4.4 COUNSELOR

73 Rutland, Mark. David The Great: Deconstructing the Man After God's Own Heart, 108.

74 Rutland, Mark. David The Great: Deconstructing the Man After God's Own Heart, 126.

75 Swindoll, Charles R.. David: A Man of Passion and Destiny, 195.

76 Swindoll, Charles R.. David: A Man of Passion and Destiny, 199.

77 Swindoll, Charles R.. David: A Man of Passion and Destiny, 204.

4.5 HUMBLED

78 Aquilina, Mike. "How the Bible Reveals the Tensions and Intentions behind the Census." Angelus. March 26, 2020. https://angelusnews.com/faith/how-the-bible-reveals-the-tensions-and-intentions-behind-the-census/.

79 Aquilina, Mike. "How the Bible Reveals the Tensions and Intentions behind the Census."

80 York, Barry. "Why David's Census Was Wrong." Gentle Reformation. March 2, 2020. https://gentlereformation.com/2020/03/02/why-davids-census-was-wrong/.

81 Phillips, Rick. "Why Was David'S Census a Great Sin?" Tenth.Org. July 28, 2002. https://www.tenth.org/resource-library/articles/why-was-davids-census-a-great-sin/.

82 Peterson, Eugene H.. First and Second Samuel, 264.

83 "Why Was God so Angry at David for Taking the Census?" Gotquestions. Org. https://www.gotquestions.org/David-census.html.

84 Peterson, Eugene H.. First and Second Samuel.

5.1 FOOLISH

85 Lucado, Max. Facing Your Giants: A David and Goliath Story for Everyday People (United States: W Publishing Group, 2006), 143.

86 Swindoll, Charles R.. David: A Man of Passion and Destiny, 133-135.

87 Peterson, Eugene H.. First and Second Samuel, 246.

88 Swindoll, Charles R.. David: A Man of Passion and Destiny, 182.

89 Lucado, Max. Facing Your Giants: God Still Does the Impossible (United States: Thomas Nelson, 2020), 144.

5.2 HUMBLED

90   Peterson, Eugene H.. First and Second Samuel, 180.

91   Swindoll, Charles R.. David: A Man of Passion and Destiny, 182-183.

92   Peters, Angie. The Life of David (United States: Thomas Nelson, 2008.)

93   Brown, Raymond. Skillful Hands: Studies in the Life of David (United States: Christian Literacy Crusade, 1972.)

94   Lucado, Max. Facing Your Giants: God Still Does the Impossible, 125.

95   Nelson, Thomas. NIV, Lucado Encouraging Word Bible: Holy Bible, New International Version (United States: Thomas Nelson, 2020.)

96   Lucado, Max. Facing Your Giants: God Still Does the Impossible, 125-126.

97   Swindoll, Charles R.. David: A Man of Passion and Destiny, 194.

98   Swindoll, Charles R.. David: A Man of Passion and Destiny, 193.

5.3 PASSIVE

99   Peterson, Eugene H.. First and Second Samuel, 191.

100 Peterson, Eugene H.. First and Second Samuel.

101 Peterson, Eugene H.. First and Second Samuel.

5.4 ABSENT

102 Whyte, Alexander. Bible Characters (United Kingdom: Oliphant Anderson and Ferrier, 1906.)

103 Peterson, Eugene H.. First and Second Samuel.

104 Peterson, Eugene H.. First and Second Samuel, 195.

105 Peterson, Eugene H.. First and Second Samuel, 196.

106 Peterson, Eugene H.. First and Second Samuel, 198.

107 Peterson, Eugene H.. First and Second Samuel, 202.

108 Peterson, Eugene H.. First and Second Samuel, 200.

109 Peterson, Eugene H.. First and Second Samuel, 201.

110 Peterson, Eugene H.. First and Second Samuel, 201.

6.1 CALCULATED

111 Kirsch, Jonathan. King David: The Real Life of the Man Who Ruled Israel, 240.

112 Stanley, Andy. "David." (Series).

113 Stanley, Andy. "David." (Series).

6.2 DECISION

114 Kirsch, Jonathan. King David: The Real Life of the Man Who Ruled Israel, 271.

115 Kirsch, Jonathan. King David: The Real Life of the Man Who Ruled Israel, 272.

116 Kirsch, Jonathan. King David: The Real Life of the Man Who Ruled Israel, 275.

6.3 EVEN THOUGH

117 Stanley, Andy. "David." (Series).

118 Stanley, Andy. "David." (Series).

119 Giglio, Louie. Don't Give the Enemy a Seat at Your Table: It's Time to Win the Battle of Your Mind... (United States: Thomas Nelson, 2021), 19.

6.4 SUCCESSION

120 Briscoe, D. Stuart. David, a Heart for God (United States: Victor Books, 1984), 169.